NORWAY
Land of Midnight Sun

(Travelogue of Norway)

Ameer Abro

Table of Contents

About the Author

Ameer Abro was born in Hala, a small town of Southern Pakistan. He acquired his primary and secondary education in his hometown. He passed his Civil Engineering from Mehran University of Engineering and Technology Jamshoro and did his master's from Norway in Port and Coastal Engineering. Apart from his Engineering background he is a writer, social worker, and a politician. His first book was his short stories and a novelette in Sindhi, published in Pakistan and his second book was a collection of newspaper articles about current affairs, published in Pakistan.

White doing his masters in Norway, he wrote his travel story expressing his feelings about Norwegian life. He travels through Rivers, fjords, historical cities and meets with various poets, social workers, students, and professors making dialogue with them about culture of Norway.

As a student of NORAD, he was travelling through the ports of Norway and enjoying the music of waves, translating them in his poetic prose, which ultimately have become a book which is in your hands now. Those who are traveling to Norway, this book is not only informative for them but also is translating observations of a sensitive human being from the third world.

Apart from his book writing, he has established a charity to send out of school children to school in Sindh, the southern province of Pakistan. He has established 33 schools where about 5000 children are enrolled from an atmosphere of no access to education.

Presently he lives in London and works with NHS as a clinical coding assistant at various surgeries maintained by NHS. He has also established a charity in UK with the name Indus Education Foundation, with the objective that he will provide educational facilities in the affected regions of Asia, Europe, and Africa.

The Gloomy Entrance

The Earth is a sphere. Many people of different colors having a thirst to see different oceans and a desire to see different countries, counting the tide of time, meet each other, touch each other, and want to know each other. In fact the total mankind have a genetic urge to experience each other. There is an eternal desire inside a man to know about different cultures, social and domestic 'problems, weather and history. I have always felt that this man, who lives inside us, wants to analyze 'at which peak of the universe is my culture standing?' He wants to compare his culture with those of others and wants to balance himself there. That's why the philosophy of Shah Latif, the great Sindhi poet suits one in every walk of life as given in the following poem:

"Always I should seek my love, but I should never achieve it"

The earth is a sphere and she has landed me over the land of mountains, Norway, the way to North. The day I arrived at the airport of its capital, Oslo, by experiencing the deep silence there, I felt, a devil would have lived here. I thought no one will ever talk to me, and that everybody was selfish. The sensitive heart which I brought from a warm land would find no friend here, would have no warmth of love. At that time, I felt that the ten months period would become a long time to stay here. Suddenly, I looked at the two heavy suitcases for which I had already paid extra money. 'It would be a big loss if I go back and pay extra money again for the reason that I felt silent at the airport of Oslo'. I thought very quickly and imagined about those friends and relatives who would laugh at me. Besides it was a fact that for a normal Pakistani, it was hard to leave his country for higher studies. However, I was not checked by customs at Oslo airport although I was accompanied with total four items excluding me. I had arrived from Karachi to Amsterdam, went to

London from over there and came back to Amsterdam a night before. The whole night I spent at the airport lounge on a sofa because the hotel at the airport was equal to 3000 rupees (700 kroner). I was given a pillow and blanket by airport authorities for free hence I preferred to save money during the travel. When they did not check my baggage at Oslo, I felt relieved there wouldn't be any robbery or smuggling in this country, however my face was giving an impression of ill-famed South Asia region for its illegal narcotics business. Later it pained me to learn that much of the narcotics Mafia was established and their business maintained in Europe although Norway had a very strict law to control this illicit trade. The university, where I was going to study, is in Trondheim. It is only an hour's flight from Oslo. A young girl in her teens was sitting beside me on the plane. She was going to see her parents in Norway. Here you will find many couples where the father is a Norwegian and the woman will be from other country. She can be a Britisher or even an American. They would prefer to live in Norway because there would be no better world other than Norway for lovers. Many people don't like severe cold and snow, especially those who come from warm countries, but I think those in love are generally playful and adventurous. Britishers are much disciplined in their habits and Norwegians are free minded. But they will not initiate in conversation with others. Due to such traditional calmness in Norwegian people, foreigners think that they are narrowing minded, although it's not true. When you will make friends then it will be felt like a sticker which I found in the centrum (the center of city) of Trondheim. It reads:

"Let the people build their skins from their own meat."

The girl, traveling with me on the plane, was going to meet her parents after six years. Her father was her stepfather, but she was going to see her real mother. Her mother had divorced her English husband and was married to a Norwegian. The girl was now living in England with her father according to court's decision. "My mother and father are very good friends although they are divorced." She spoke. I am not surprised to listen such a story because I had read a lot of books about the marital life in the west, although I am curious to know the reasons why they separate from each other in a short time. In Norway, the ratio of divorce and marriage is almost same, my friend Andres in the Trondheim University was also living with his mother whose current husband is not his father. He told me that it was usual in Norway, and they consider it every body's right to choose or reject his or her partner. "To beat a woman in Asian countries is not considered a crime. Divorce in the same way is not taken as a stigma." He once said. Although his observation was not correct that to beat a woman in Pakistan was not considered a bad thing. It is considered a bad practice, but nobody bothers to pinpoint such cases of a male and nobody can finger him in the society. In Norway, a person accused of beating of his wife would be charged with at least 25000 Kroner (US $ 2420.0) as fine. Trondheim is the third largest city in Norway, build in the cradle of hills, rivers and, the seaside but its population is only 140,000. I already expected that while landing at the airport, I would feel as if I had landed on Larkana airport (a small city in Pakistan). The airport, built in the cradle of hills is small but beautiful. It fascinates the newcomers. Going to the university from the airport, the green hills and small houses are seen in array. The SAS (Scandinavian air system) bus left us at the hotel Royal Garden, where the social secretary of NORAD, Turid, welcomed us and soon we were engaged in informal conversation. Meanwhile many students from India and Sri Lanka assembled along with Pakistani students and all of us were led to Moholt (student town). One of my suitcases was lost due to chaos and confusion. I was disturbed by this loss and followed the points where I had been short while before but couldn't find the case.

"Don't worry, you will get your suitcase." Everyone was offering such sympathetic remarks when I asked them to do something practical, I found them simply indifferent. 'What a silly people they are!' I thought and remembered the time when my brother's brand-new car but small was stolen in Karachi only a few days ago and we couldn't find it despite of police reporting and bringing the matter into notice of the inspector general. There wasn't any valuable document in the case, but I had brought some household items from Pakistan after knowing that living in Norway was expensive and, all those articles were kept in that suitcase. I opened the telephone diary, which was given by the social secretary, and in a hurry dialed a lot of numbers but couldn't find any clue of the suitcase. At last, with the broken heart, I came to my hostel room and found the suitcase lying there! I thought I had been haunted by a sense of insecurity in previous days but now I felt relaxed and had a sound sleep. After two days, we were brought to Ringve museum of music. We had arrived in Norway in August hence there were still some glimpses of summer, a season in which there was no heat and perspiration. Summer in Europe means bright sunshine and long days. We, while in younger days would laugh at white men having sunbathe at Karachi beach in summer. We came to know why the summer was so important for these people having lived a whole winter here. Ringve was the first museum of music; I have had ever seen in my life. This was entirely different museum as compared to other museums of culture and history. It was creative. There were musical instruments from almost each part of the world. A technical system was arranged inside it; rooms inside rooms were built in such a way as if there were boxes put inside boxes, found from the deep sea. If you tirade the lands?" First, he couldn't understand my question but later after roper understanding he replied with a sense of pride; "We don't have the image of feudalism like Germans and East Europeans. This country believes in equality. The only owners of those lands are the farmers who worked on them." I realized that the Norwegians were very proud of their advanced culture. They won't be compared with any of world's nations as they could be called cruel or feudal. The Germans ruled here for four years during the peak time of Hitler hence Norwegians hated their culture. It was also observed that they are very conservative in respect to language and currency like the Germans, French and Japanese. Even English knowing students wanted their courses to be taught in Norsk. Therefore a few courses and those funded by NORAD were taught in English. The foreigners were bound to take a language course and then enter in their MSc courses. If you open a bank account in Norwegian currency (kroner), you will get the interest otherwise you can't open the account in dollars in a Norwegian bank with interest. You can only open an account in foreign currency in international banks like City Bank, American Express Bank and enjoy the interest. The Prime Minister of Norway is a woman reigning since the last five years and was also in power before this term. There are fourteen political parties in the country. Most of them are committed to social work for example taking care of old peoples' rights and some others safeguarding the rights of music lovers. Rests of them are purely concerned with political affairs. The Prime Minister hails from labor party but I had not seen any long rally in Norway yet. Also, I don't think there would be any special protocol for the Prime Minister or a royal palace to reside. The royal family, the descendant from King Olav, has separate houses in every large city, so that they could live with comfort, enjoying their picnics and cycle rides. Herald-V who dons the royal crown these days was born on 21st February 1937 and was crowned on 17th January 1991. The royal couple has two children, the son Haakon was born on 20th June 1973 and the daughter Martha Luis on 22nd September 1997. We went to see the city's top view after our visit to cultural museum was over. The green color of Cathedral building is very huge and imposing in the city. Trondheim was at least 500 feet below from the place where we were standing at that time. Many buildings were to be seen from there. The TV tower is also an important sight to be seen from the top. Half of this country is covered with hills, glaciers, fountains and rivers. The other half is populated. Almost all the cities are built on hills. It is known that in older days, the whole country was covered with snow. As times passed, the snow melted, and the place became habitable. Uprooted people from different parts of the world started coming over there and got settled. There were enough jobs for them. Slowly they built this country, and it is now counted among the most developed countries of the world. After glancing the top view of Trondheim, we went to the Cathedral where the priest and guide informed us about the different structures found in the Cathedral. There are statues of Christ in the museum, having different colors built in different archaeological modes. Miriam beside Christ is invariably seen in every statue. Boys and girls, half-clad are seen seated on benches freely kissing each other. Unlike us they don't have any moral restrictions from their religion and parents. Most people go to worship on Sundays only. People go to Churches, sit there and listen to religious music or read Bible in separate room. On returning, we also listened to that music which started from a very soft tune but ended in a very exhausted mode with so much excitement. The song would mean a separate meaning but whenever, I listen to any strange music, I seek some feeling in its background and if I reach to some conclusion, I feel satisfied.

Poland was about 26 million in those times. He informed me about some Polish authors. I could only recognize the name of "Coleridge" from them. He told me about one Polish Noble Prize Winner writer; Mitoshi. The poetess was awarded the Nobel Prize in 1983 and now lives in Los Angles. Martin was an adventurous man; he had come to Norway driving his car from Poland. He had acquired expertise on driving through the Norwegian hilly tracks but had a problem that he couldn't park his car for more than 8 hours in the city. The parking rent for the whole day was so light that he would lose the entire amount of his scholarship if he kept it parking. I advised him to buy a secondhand bicycle from the market (the Lope market). He agreed and next day we both went to a Lope market. We discussed about many literary and political issues in our way to lope market. He told me that he had an interest in reading and writing but he was unable to write anything. However, he believed that a person could better express in his own language. He bought a bicycle in good order. As we were coming back, a Norwegian family called him and said, "Can you sell this bicycle in 300 kroner?" Martin found it a tempting offer and sold the bicycle on second call of those Norwegians because he had purchased that it in only 210 Kroner. We laughed and returned on foot. "It was not a good decision to sell the bicycle." I spoke. "It was a very good business and, I can claim now that once I rode a Norwegian cycle." The rate of currency in Poland was very low. He calculated and told me that 100 Norwegian kroner were equal to 3250 mocha (Polish currency) and, his pay in Poland was equal to 1250 kroner while in Pakistan, the pay of a 17-grade officer was equal to about 2000 kroner. Here we were paid 7000 kroner by Norad, and only single persons were able to save money from that allowance, but it was hard to survive living with a family in that allowance. However, Norway was the most expensive country even considering the conditions in other Scandinavian countries where only to travel in bus for one side, cost 14 kroner.

The next day was Friday, we thought of enjoying a Norwegian disco and went there. We sat there for quite a long time. Many of the girls were half clad seen in the arms of their boyfriends and were gossiping with each other. A Norwegian came and engaged me in conversation, "In Pakistan and India, do girls marry by their own will?" he asked. "Yes" I said, "but not always and everywhere." His question led me to think that no society could be measured from its outwardly image. Free sex in Norwegian society certainly did not mean "Free for all" having sex with any one at any time. Those people had a separate history of social development, ethics, morality, and sense of freedom. That sense of freedom was not only related with sex but it was basically related with free will. After all that man was critical of Pakistani society from the women's point of view being denied freedom like in the western society. He said, "There is no fun in life if you ask a girl to dance and she reports to the police." Simply I smiled said, "You also divorce your wife soon after the marriage. The rate of marriage and divorce is the same in Norway." "People don't marry very often here. We don't think, love only means wearing a ring, however it depends on man's will. If he couldn't live with someone; why should he live to suffer?" He spoke. However, it was a deeper issue to be discussed. He offered us some beer, may be because he was drunk, or he was treating us as guests. He said, "Enjoy Yourself." Martin had already brought some beer from his room. We were drinking at a table. We both didn't have any girlfriend hence were sitting like cigarette puffs thrown on the pathway. I could have never approached any girl without some emotional appeal or attachment. To offer a woman a kiss and a sex was a fashion here and, I was drunk hence I could follow that fashion. When many seminude girls come close to me than an ambitious human being from my insight desired to touch them. A girl clads in blue came near me and started talking about the same old debate; "There is a lot of gender difference in Pakistan?" I was sick of that question put to me so often while my stay in Norway. Personally, I have never discriminated between man and woman and would not favor such conduct. I have spent a free and independent life in a country like Pakistan despite of its conservative society. Whenever and with whom so ever, I have been in love, I have loved her with full involvement avoiding the society's restrictions. I like the shyness in a woman if it's natural. I can't reject that shyness just because the woman is not active in life or is not progressive, but I love her originality. I adore that smile which is virgin. I love those girls who want to conceal their stormy emotions of love facing a crowd. That girl's name was Curry, incidentally that was same as my grandmother's name. She said, "One of my friends lived in Islamabad, her father was working in Swiss Embassy, hence wrote me in one of her letters that no one could go out in miniskirts in this city!" "Forget Pakistan, tell me something about yourself" I asked her. I was watching only the pink and blue shades in her dress; pink was her skin color and blue was the color of her short suit. I think Norwegian girls don't wear braziers hence their breasts are attractive, as they are open to the delight of all young men, nothing to hide. "We are two sisters and a brother. Mother and father are also in the house. Every week one person has to clean the house and one has to cook the food for the whole week. In this way we distribute our work. Nobody can interfere in other's life. I am studying at the University and my whole day is spent with friends. There is freedom of sex in our society." I was waiting for the last pronouncement. I thought if the ambitious man in me was alive then I should have understood the meaning of that sentence. She kept on talking but I couldn't listen, it was all meaningless. I was excited and wanted to pull her into my arms and kiss her but there was some fear stored from my thirty years Pakistani life where even to talk with a girl is an act of suspicion. I was steering through her bare breasts like a hungry cat at a meat shop till the end but couldn't say; 'if she was agreed to go with me to a room; I could arrange some beer for her'. She left instead of sitting in my boring company. I bounced again with Martin in that Norwegian disco. Martin was talking about western music and, I was nodding, 'yes' or 'No'. While coming back, I put my hands in Curry's arms with courage and said, "Do you like to stay with me tonight?" "At present, I am feeling sleepy, may be at other time." She said and ran away with her complete bewitching sexual appeal.

Trondheim A Lovely City

Next weekend, we went to see the student union office. At the union office, I thought, we would meet some student leaders who would inform us about the problems of the fellow students' crucial issues to be discussed with university bosses. Since we were the least concerned with their problems, I thought we shouldn't go there but later presumed it would be a good outing. As the student union office (called student Sam fondant) was in the city, I would also take a glimpse of the city while coming back. But at the union office I found a totally different atmosphere. The auditorium was bustling with the students, and the stage nicely decorated. It was a welcome program for this year's new students. As commonly seen at the universities in Pakistan, singers are invited at such occasions and place lavishly decorated. But at the University of Trondheim, students themselves decorate the meeting hall, although a stage was already there providing a built-in facility to perform any type of celebration. The stage was a mobile one, could also move around. Three sets at a time could be set on it. A room inside the hall meticulously controlled the lighting arrangement. There was a huge area behind the stage, divided into different sections of dance, music, acting, and magazine and of volunteers, etc. every year the students were selected after an interview to be placed in a department. Every student took part in this activity free of cost and without making any payment. I have never seen such a wonderful system of entertainment in Pakistan made by students themselves. The program was conducted in Norse therefore a foreigner like me could only follow those portions, which were based on action and movement and not on dialogues. The viewers in hall were laughing but the people from Pakistan, Sri Lanka, India and of African countries were looking with black faces like fools, just laughing without comprehending anything. There was only one action, which I could follow. The central idea of that scene was to show the cultural difference between the year 1910 and 1994. Scene one: (1910) a girl was swimming in a river and her clothes were hanging on the branch of a tree. Some naughty boys take away her clothes and she kept waiting for her clothes to get them back. She called a teacher at the bridge who covered her bare body with his jacket. The students who stole the clothes were dismayed. Scene Two: (1994) two boys were wandering in a park. They saw some girls around. They offered them a kiss and asked them to show their breasts. The girls put off their shirts and showed them the breasts for a short time. In the evening they are shown dancing and kissing in the disco. Both the skits showed the difference between the cultural attitudes of the young men in the year 1910 and 1994. The stage is part of their culture, every foreigner is surprised to see that when he comes here, he suddenly becomes excited. Nudity is not prohibited in the whole Europe and America. In some countries, it is part of their culture. For the Norwegians, free sex is common, but they become conscious if a foreigner makes fun of that freedom. They won't bear their freedom to be disgraced. Norway is still not the member of European Union. Many years ago, a referendum was held here in the country on this question, but most of the people voted not to join EU. They were afraid of losing their freedom by doing so. By the end of the year 1994, the government planned to hold another referendum because it favored joining it to acquire trade benefits. The Norwegians are self-centered people indifferent towards the problems of other people. To me this attitude was quite disturbing. If you ever start talking about the issues of Bosnia or Rwanda with a common man, he will say, "I see!" This was the degree of their ignorance about world affairs. Nevertheless, they live happily, work hard and are concerned only with their own matters. This attitude was found in them because as students they were engaged in only particular subject. The other reason not to bother about world affairs was the social security system in the country, according to which no one was concerned with the political merits and demerits of the land. The next day we went for fishing along the Trondheim fjord. Fjord is the name of an area, covered with hills and seawater runs through those hills. Somewhere beautiful waterfalls and fountains are found while wandering through those fjords. Passing through any fjord, colorful landscapes fuel the soul with vitality and wets the dry eyes which, I had brought from the dried lands of Sindh. Norway is among a few countries of the world where one can find fjords. There are 280 fjords, 200 small rivers and 20 big rivers in Norway hence this whole country is richly adorned with nature. To travel along the Trondheim fjord is like giving a white flower of hope in a basket to an innocent child especially in spring. The ferry took us at 6 O'clock in the evening. It was a small ferry in which there was a single small cabin of 20 seats and an open deck. A small island was seen from the place we left, smaller than Manora (in Karachi) but more beautiful than our island. The hills were seen around and Trondheim city in the east, from where I could see the only red tram passing at every ten minutes. Clean and sky-blue seawater and cool air were most pleasant to nerves of the body therefore they pulled me towards a corner of the deck. I tried to fill my heart with colorful beauty of the universe. A lost man from the land of mysticism, keeping a lot of desires in his heart had reached at a corner of the North to struggle and make a living. "Is there any route linked to any part of the world from here, where nature has some end? Are there any more colors of nature, I have to see as yet?" I thought for a while. In the meantime, a pinkish light covered the sky. The sun was to lie in the hills, many people with happy faces were roaming on the deck. There were some sad faces as well with the bottles of bear in their hands, gazing in the dying shadows of the sun and its reflection in the sea. The sun was kissing their sad faces and that pink light reminded me of the land where I was born! After some time, the ferry stopped at a deeper point and everybody threw his string in the sea. One of our teachers found a hefty fish after several failed attempts. Everybody applauded in cheers. The teacher pulled his string hurriedly and took out the trembling fish out of water. During that part of the year when we visited Trondheim fjord, the sunset time was between 11.00 to 230. It was an autumn evening hence sunset time was about 9 O'clock. After the fishing was over, we cooked the fish. It was delicious so we enjoyed it till midnight.

Norwegian Hills

After some days our course leader took us to his cabin which was built up in the hills. Professor Eivind Bratteland which means "height of the land", had traveled throughout world. Now he was the leader of our course, "Port and Coastal engineering", a course he has been teaching since many years. Before our visit to his cabin, he took us to see the highest ski jump in Trondheim. What a jump it would be! I thought. Skiing is the game, which is played on snow and is Norway's national game. Norway is most often winner of all the World Championships in skiing. This game is mostly played in winter because of thick snow, but they have made a plastic jump in Trondheim as well so that they could go for skiing in spring and summer also. The highest jump of the World is 210 meters, in Czechoslovakia. The jump in Trondheim is 120 meters high and to reach that, one has to climb a staircase up to 500 feet. "The person who reaches at the top and come back first, will get a very sweet chocolate from me." The professor announced. All the people went up in slow pace but were tired halfway. A student from South American country, Peru was going with his wife but his wife sat down half way and he kept on going. When I reached the last part of stairs, there was no energy in my legs. But the professor at 54 years age old was coming back after touching the top. "Don't take too much time upstairs because we have to go further." He said to me while coming back. I lost the rest of energy left in legs because I was thinking to take a few minutes rest on the top. When I reached the top, the jump was looking longer than it is expected from the down and, I was thinking about those person's courage who jump from here and play with their lives. If a Sindhi does this kind of dangerous move and his mother comes to know about it, she will immediately stop her son from going out. Breathing heavily when we came back and sat in the car; the professor said, "The next exercise is four times strenuous than this one! "Oh, no!" everybody cried. The professor took us into the hills, some 40 km away from Trondheim, where we had to climb up in the hills towards his summer cabin. We saw the system of burning the waste material on the way. The garbage taken from big boxes through the vehicles is left there, where a plant is installed which kills all the bacteria carried by the garbage, which could produce pollution. I was surprised to see the smoke coming out of a pipe of that plant which was whiter than the clouds! We were going with professor Bratteland, his wife and a mixed couple from Norway and Philippine, the similar couple I had seen in Trondheim in which a Philippine woman was married to a Norwegian. She came to attend the same course in 1989 and married a Norwegian, named, Jani. Now she only goes to meet her parents every year in the Philippines. A couple of days ago, I had seen a Philippine woman, working in a bank. She was also married to a Norwegian. Marriage is a very individual act. When someone falls in love, he leaves behind his national and cultural bounds quite often but love and marriage also is related with religion perhaps that's why I never saw a Muslim woman, marrying a Norwegian. Since the Philippines are Christians and worship along with other nationals, they can do it without changing their religion. Another factor is that the Philippine society is a free society with a very few restrictions. A girl from Philippine now in Moholt is NORAD fellow and her husband lives in Philippine. She has three children and lives in this country without fear and sense of insecurity. She is always well dressed, makes friends and moves about everywhere. As against this, if a Muslim male had to leave his wife alone in a country like Norway, he would have passed hundreds of suspicious, sleepless nights. And after leaving her, he would have developed some other complexes. However, Jani took us into the hills. The professor's cabin was one km high from the place we started which passed away. There was a beautiful landscape with a lake, seen from his cabin. The lake, a nature's gift in the middle of the hills awoke from a long sleep, the love for nature in my soul. In Norway, I have felt a pressing desire to be a painter. I wish God had given me a remote control so that I could touch it and become an artist! The artist can paint any natural beauty using colors. The natural beauties of the world can't be well translated into words. They reflect the feelings without words and those feelings could be well translated through unique paintings. Was it possible that the beauty of this lake could be summed up into a single painting? It could be translated either in one painting or couldn't be depicted even in one thousand paintings!

We walked a little bit further and saw the lake from a height of another 100 ft. By then, the lake had changed her face and looked like a dancer who changes her dress after each song and dance on another one. I saw the dance of the lake from different views and enjoyed it. The professor had a stick in his hand like advocates and was really looking true to his name, 'height of land'. "There is a lake after every 5 km in the hills and we call it a small sea. There are sometimes small power plants beside those lakes which are dug 500 feet down the hill" Professor told the students. This country has taken the benefit from a great supply of water and has built small dams and power plants. There is no dispute here like Kala Bagh dam issue in Pakistan. Everybody works here on his own subject and is sincere, keeping the national cause in mind. Pakistan could also make small power plants in Kalam and Kagan valley. Some power plants along with the River Indus in Pakistan could also be built, leaving aside the Kalabagh issue. By seeing the development in these countries, I always question the wisdom of our people. How far away are we from the present position of the world? These people have learned to love their land and, they are very close to the real issues of their countries. We don't have the real concept of love in collective matters. I must have derived an inspiration for Pakistan after seeing this country!

We reached further and the professor said, "There is still a walk of two hours ahead." The mouths of students kept open for a small moment. We looked around in horror with gaping mouths. "How old are you?" I asked the professor. "54 years." "Do you come to this cabin at every weekend?" "No, we usually come here in winter when the trees are covered with snow." He said, pointing towards the forest into the hills, pointing towards the lake, he said, "And when this lake turns into snow, we come to the cabin while skiing, spend a comforting night and return the next day." By saying these words, he looked lovingly his wife. When we reached the top of that mountain, he gave two alternatives to the students whether we could go further and make tea and coffee along with the lake or cook something here at a pond. I was surprised how could we cook there but then I recalled the travelogues of Vasco de Gama and Ibn Batoota and could recall many ways of cooking along a river. I thought there would be some material in the bag hanging on the back of professor or there would be a cylinder of gas in it but that didn't happen. Everyone gave consent to cook beside the nearest pond. So we were asked to collect dry woods. We collected some sticks, and the professor took out two kettles, some bags of tea, milk and, sugar from his bag. Everybody took out the food and beer they had brought from their homes and started eating rather gulping: Everybody was hungry after a tiring long walk! Suddenly the professor's friend Jani announced to every one's surprise and said, "You know, today is the birthday of Professor Bratteland and, he will cut the cake." He took out a cake and 54 candles from his bag. "Oh! You have brought all this stuff with you with so much care?" exclaimed the professor. Both the wife and husband sat along a tree and looked to be happy. They were presented with the cake and candles. He cut the cake, and everyone sang, "Happy birthday to you." In fact in South Asian society, people commonly remind their friends of birthdays, quite suddenly to give him a surprise. As I remember when I was passing through a tragic phase of my life due to the death of my wife in an accident, a good friend of mine sent me a bunch of flowers on my birthday. I really came out of tears finding the flowers. At that moment I felt deep love for the person and was assured about the existence of love in the world. I don't know what the feelings of the professor were but I could see a shade of pathos on the face of this Norwegian old man and thought that the people of this land don't suffer the sorrows of inner life the way we do. While coming back, we stopped at the professor's cabin for some time where we all took out the bottles of beer from their bags and offered them to the professor. Professor took a bottle and started drinking with a relish. The wife recalled the professor, "You should not drink, and you have yet to drive." Of course, it is an offense if someone drives while drunk. "I can drive the car if you like so." I offered. "Do you think that it is a bottle of Fanta in your hands?" said the professor's wife pointing towards the beer bottle in my hands. Everybody laughed. The lady from Philippine, Jani's wife was also cutting jokes with her husband, "You should also not drink too much. Have you checked your weight?" He kept smiling and drinking without giving any answer. People usually avoid drinking whisky and wine here because these are expensive. In bigger parties also, they offer beer after only one peg of wine or whisky. "What should be his weight now?" I asked. "88 Kilograms." Replied the

Philippine woman her name is very difficult to pronounce, and I don't even now remember. "And age? Because weight is judged according to a person's age and height?" I asked. "That you have to guess, and anybody can guess." She spoke. Everybody looked at Jani's body and height intently. Some said 30 years, some said 25 years and, some 35, but we were surprised to hear that he was 45 years old. Considering the country's climate, everyone looks young. Some days later that Philippine woman met me in downtown. I was curious to know as to why Asian and African people prefer to marry the westerners, so I asked some searching questions. "I have worked for 15 years in the Philippine, but I can't get a job even if I have done a course in NTH." "Then it seems that you married quite late." She smiled at my question and didn't reply. I was expecting that she had already got married in the Philippine but not so. She fell in love when she met Jani in Norway, hence she left all her family behind. "I sacrificed a lot. Not only I have left my high-level job but left my children also. Now since my husband is here and I live with him. I miss my parents deeply. It is not easy to go there for a short visit." We were standing in a Lope market, which was arranged to save the nature. Although Trondheim is a beautiful city, they think that in comparison with other cities of Norway, this is more polluted and, birds and plants are not properly fed here. I was surprised to hear it. I had thought that they had got everything including nature, beauty except spiritual love but they love to preserve nature. I was wandering in my own dreams. The Philippine woman left saying 'goodbye' because she had to meet her husband.

First Trip to Oslo

I made a program to see Oslo, so I left Trondheim in the night and, reached Oslo at 730 a.m. Oslo is the only international port in Norway from where the trains start their journey to everywhere in Europe. In Europe, there is a train system, called Inter Rail, by which students can travel on concessional rates. Another train of the same kind is called Euro Train. There were only 1012 people in my compartment. Of them many of them were army people. As I was going to Oslo from Trondheim, I thought they had to report on duty in early morning. People observe the punctuality here and transport is available to everyone in abundance. Perhaps it was the reason why the night train was going almost empty. I was reading, sleeping side by side and snoring for the whole night in the compartment. Although by looking at the moon through trees at Trondheim railway station, I felt the moon was also very lonely and that's why it was looking so depressed. The solitude in Norway has left the nature on its way. Oslo is a beautiful city for a traveler seeking a quiet life. Here there are more than 12 museums, 5 art galleries, a beautiful fjord and very big shopping centers. The population is more than four lacks therefore some crowd was seen around. I saw a very small portion of the city in a single day's transport ticket of 35 Kroner. In this ticket, one could travel in a Ferry, Tram, Bus, Underground train, and any other transport. I was traveling through the Oslo fjord and steered at the sea in the cradle of hills. One Norwegian couple was sitting in front of me. "Do you have any interest in religion?" One of them asked me. "What do you mean?" I don't always understand such question because I think one's own faith is involved while choosing the religion. Every body's perception steers through the glass of every religion by his own means and incidents. Due to these contradictions, the world has faced and is facing the crucial splits among different communities. That topic is not the name of any food so that I could express my interest! However, the eyes of that couple were twinkling and I guessed that the shinning was not the shining of dance, music, and drink. "Have you ever thought that the humans have left the religion?" the girl asked. "To remember and to forget God starts from an image and that image, I have not seen in

Norwegian people." She took out some literature from her purse and handed it over to me. "I don't understand that language." I spoke. "What language you understand?" she asked. "English." I said and was thinking that if she doesn't have any book in English then it is impossible to find a book in Urdu too. "Actually, I don't have the Bible in English." The holy book she was asking about clearly indicated that she was a Christian. The Christians believe that the Christ was the Son of God and didn't move further. It is correct that the very few people were seen in Churches and Cathedrals in most of the European countries. The religion doesn't leave any good impression on their lives hence it was not necessary to discuss religion in this society but by considering the nature of western society, finding a couple preaching religion was like a miracle to me. Personally, I felt love for them. Such an innocent, friendly and loving couple talking about religion was not expected by me while traveling along the fjord. "I can speak and understand Urdu too." There were more than 20,000 Pakistanis in Oslo, who were mostly labors living since last 2025 years. I felt sorry and not guilty to saying that robbery, smuggling, and cheating was not uncommon among the South Asians, and I knew that there was an association of Urdu speaking people which had organized publishing newspapers and, magazines also. When I told her about Urdu, she said, "You give me your address and I will send you the books in Urdu." I didn't tell her until the end that I was a Muslim because it was unnecessary to inform about it. If I had told her about my religion, she would never have come forward and tell me about herself. This is a great truth for me that religion has taught me the lessons of humanity that's why after reading the lesson of humanity in the eyes of that man and woman, I felt happy and spent the day, in a pleasant mood. After leaving the ferry, I went to see Norway's National gallery where I could find the old coins, handicrafts, cultural garments, and sculptures. I was not surprised because leaving aside some places, people don't wear cultural or traditional clothes normally. People are seen well-dressed mostly on Sundays in front of Churches. For example, if a child is born, there is a tradition that the priest will pour the water first time in the child's mouth at a Church ceremony. People wear ceremonial dresses at that function. The marriages can be held in the presence of 45 people in any house or Church and can be registered. They don't waste their time upon marriages. They are surprised to hear about our ceremonies where marriages take around seven days. The groom at the occasion would be on leave for at least a month from his office. The boys, girls and children would stay in groom's house and would be singing with a thumping African drum. The old women would be sitting all the time in the kitchen. The problem is not of unnecessary hassle but is of a long-time tradition. Cultural events. are the part of joy, which lies in the breast of contemporary society. An American can call it ultra-modern if he enjoys the typical day to day clothing and dance. But it may not be enjoyable to an Arab, who enjoys his moments of joy in a Caber dance. Hence culture often differs from person to person and then from society to society. I wanted to see the National theatre but there was a construction work going on, therefore I went ahead to the King's place. I had to reach the airport at 5 O'clock in the evening to receive my wife. It was 230 now. To see any huge museum, more time was needed so to while away some moments, I wandered in the center of city, walking aimlessly. Every color is seen here, especially the people from the subcontinent are found everywhere in Oslo. Women are usually seen with their children especially Pakistani and Indian women. Suddenly the sun came out and twinkled over people's faces. I was wandering at the bus terminal of Oslo, which has 30 platforms inside, from where one could go anywhere in Europe by road. Sunshine here is like clouds in Pakistan when people like to go to the beaches. When sunshine touches the body here, one feels as if a beautiful girl is soothing the whole body with tenderness. The railway station is exactly in front of the bus terminal. I went and sat with couples sitting calmly at outside railway station to enjoy the sunshine. A couple who had a bag of books with them was asking some questions to people every time and offering the book also. I thought it is a special thing. Earlier I guessed the girl is hunting the boys and the boys were hunting the girls, but later laughed at my thought. We travel in Europe with this view that the boys and girls going on the ways are looking only for each other. This couple was selling a dictionary of guidelines to get social rights in Norway. They had published it on their own expenses. The book was in Norse so I couldn't follow it but by looking.at some pictures, I could understand some rules. That if your wife's behavior with you is unworthy or nature is not preserved well in your neighbor, you are handicapped, you have some educational problems and, many such issues confront you, then the book could guide you to get your rights and that couple could also explain to you some points if you so desire. The book can guide you where to go for your problem to be solved. I found them talking to the people about their domestic problems in sincere manner. Some people didn't like to speak anything personal as in Pakistan nobody would care to hear the hawkers at railway stations. The earth is moving around sun. The time of sunrise and sunset changes rapidly in North. Someone doesn't believe in that dilemma; he will believe so if he lives here. Many days are passed, I have not seen the stars. When the moon shines at Karachi beach, I remember how the poets of Sindh recall their beloved ones and count the waves of ocean? I remember the situation; I miss it completely. I came to this village Trondheim, which they call the third largest city of Norway and, slept a pleasant night with my wife.

Historical City of Roros

There is a historical city in the west of Trondheim called Roros. I had an opportunity to visit the place. Two buses carrying NORAD students started from Trondheim, and it was raining. Rain is taken as a bad weather in Norway. Cold wind was blooming on that day. Cold wind along with the rain seemed to penetrate in the tissues of body very severely. The elements, which were impressive for a poet and writer meant the moments, which were the food for soul, and related to the climate and atmosphere. I had felt such a feeling living there. Here if I read a story, it would usually begin with the words; "It was a beautiful evening of summer." I have to write about Norwegian literature in detail but at the moment, I wish to share a song, which was sung by a tiny girl while going to Roros in the bus. I would love to tell you about the song in such a way as if it.is written in music, but words can't sing a song if they are only written on paper. The real music is always found in the chest of the singer. It was a two-hour travel and there were for some times screening of TV, cassette recorder and a mike for the tourist guide. Turid was our tourist guide, a Norwegian connected with the foreign students since last 15 years. She is very friendly too. Don't ask about her age because if you asked about the age and wanted to compare it with your countrymen's age then it would be difficult to say anything. Norwegian women look young till the age of 4050 years. Life expectancy of a woman is 79 years and of a man 71. An African girl sang this song when the sun suddenly shone, and we were going to the historical city of Roros:

Can you color the summer?

Can you color the rainbow?

Can you color the sunshine on beaches?

Can you color the lagoon on moon's night?

Can you color the heart, full of love?

Can you color the soul, full of anxiety?

The anger I had for Norwegian disco music faded away when I listened to that melody. In fact, the child's voice was so sweat that one felt the meaning in words and to me the western elements of poetry seemed beautiful and true, first time. One month had passed in Norway but the mode of thinking had not changed yet. There were mines of copper in Roros some 300 years ago, where the poor people used to work. They found about 150 tons of copper there. Denmark ruled Norway in those days and Denmark had a war with Sweden to win the Norwegian territories. The work improved in these mines because the king Of Denmark needed more copper to make weapons. We can imagine how this nation suffered during slavery and how hard they had worked, perhaps that was the reason as to why they could not tolerate the presence of foreigners on their soil. There are many mines here and the biggest mine is 1600 meters down where the temperature is minus 40 degrees C, whereas on land it is 2 degrees C. We could go only 50 meter down the mine. The system of working inside the hills is scientific. To transport the copper, a railway track was built. For laborers, eating room and a toilet were separately built. They said there were days when peasants had to work for continuously 3040 days without any break. At present these mines and museums are used as a means of revenue. There is still some quantity of copper in Norway but now they have become rich from oil export, from fish export and electricity generated from the water. In these days, the wages of a labor are so high that a minister also doesn't have servants. There is an automatic music system in mines, which is heard through cassette recorders. Those voices were the relative voices during work. Incidentally our guide woman was an American who married a Norwegian and preferred to live in this small city of Roros, but she had a true love with history and archaeological rites. She remembered not only the "full mines system" of Roros but also knew about many Norwegian historical buildings and other different metals. There was no song heard while coming back. Everyone was given a bottle of drink free of charge. I felt drowsy therefore I slept well in the bus and, when awoke, we were in Trondheim where it was still raining. A short while raining, then sunshine, intermittent raining, and sunshine, I wondered how long this will continue! When the wind blew wildly, the umbrella was straightened we soon were wet. I wondered what type of autumn it was. I had never seen a wild and crazy wind and autumn. I had never seen such original yellow colors in my country, not even felt in any poem of Shaikh Ayaz, the eminent Sindhi poet of Pakistan. I was walking with an umbrella and raincoat and looking towards the skies closely. The whole scene of pale and withered leaves flew away from heart. I was very fond of reading Norwegian folk literature to understand the society in depth. I felt there was no image of being adored in this country, but history could tell me the chain. This was strange though a stranger couldn't talk about anything beyond his profession. Since these people don't interfere into other people's personal problems, they don't have interest in an irrelevant also. The stories of mountainous locations are also related to their lifestyle, dress and social infrastructure but feelings related to human life are universally the same. I could feel more deeply about that when I met a professor who was working on the folk stories in Norway. He narrated me many folk stories recalling the good old days when people would sit in a circle intently listening to the storyteller. These were also called folk tales. Troll is an animal like bear but bigger in height. This animal is born in the mountainous locations of Norway and is presented in their culture. You will find statues, other types of sculptures of trolls presented on TV, Fridge and, on show pieces in people's homes. Parents control their noisy and rowdy children by the name of troll. "I dreamt a troll through the thick trees when I was a small kid." Professor started to tell me his dream. "Come here, I will kill you." Troll said to professor in his dream. "You must not eat me because I am too small. If you wait for some time, I will call my elder brother who is bigger than me in height. You will enjoy eating him." Professor said to troll in the dream. I liked his sense of humor. He told me that in the year 200 A.D, a story was written here in which an image of love is created. The story is like this: "A poor girl used to live with a troll in her house: When a child grows up, any pet animal obviously becomes the source of entertainment. But the troll was a very different and strange thing finding a girl riding on a dangerous animal who was living with her in a small house. Meanwhile a prince, the third and youngest son of the king developed a liking for that girl. He wore the skin of a troll on his body and used to visit her house in the night. He used to sleep with her and return back before morning. One day the girl thought of meeting her mother, who lived in another city, so she wanted the troll to go with her. The prince, the youngest son of the king thought that he should avail that opportunity and should go with her in the disguise of troll, he therefore went alone with her instead of the troll. When she reached her mother's house; the mother asked her if the troll would sleep with her in the night. The girl said yes. One night when the prince was having love with her and had undressed the troll's skin body, mother heard some strange voices from another room, lit the candle and, was surprised to see that her daughter was living with the most beautiful prince instead of the troll. The troll after seeing her love with the prince forced the king to arrange the marriage of the prince within three days. The king did the likewise and the troll was appointed to be the prince's guard. When the girl was told about Prince's marriage, she desired to meet him in the night. Troll gave sleeping pills to the prince in the first two nights hence she couldn't meet the prince for first two days. On the third night, girl was excited to sleep with the prince and reached at last despite the hindrances made by the troll. They made love with each other that night." "And what about the marriage of the prince?" I asked like a Pakistani woman when he concluded the story. "There is no connection with marriage in story but this story shows that a woman is a very active partner in love affairs and a man is quite passive." I thought of the poetry of great Sindhi poet Shah Latif, in which the image of love in a woman is stable and quite active. How a beautiful girl of Sindh called "Sohni" became rebellious in the society and crossed the river Indus to meet her lover. Sassui's long journey through deserts, the meditation of Surath and the devotion of Marvi, in most of such characters, woman is an active character in love. After wandering in many countries and studying a little their culture and history, I have felt that in such matters, the conduct of one or the other can't be demoralized. It always depends as to how the person has passed his or her life. Personally, I am a strange character when I am in love with any woman because the feeling is deep and aggressive in me. As I move in a woman with whom I am in love, it makes my mind active and hard working. I get energy from the reflection of one's personality and, then I work all day, sleep well and feel like always being with her. Perhaps I pass each and every moment in love when I am certain of my emotions. In today's Norwegian society, it is rare to hear the idioms such as dreams, soul and, religion hence since many years, a gap is felt in country's spiritual life. In every society, there are people who take care of their spiritual needs and if they don't get the spiritual food then they move towards such desperate actions that the void becomes very difficult to be filled. After all habits also tell mostly about one's behavior. People in general have a habit of living with dogs here; they are fond of keeping them in their company and to wander with them. It is a common scene the husband sitting on the back seat and dog on the front seat. When I was coming from Amsterdam to Oslo, I met a man who was coming from United States. He told me that he went to the States to purchase a dog, but he didn't like it. He had seen the advertisement of a dog in a paper. I thought I should have brought some dogs from Pakistan where they are loafing in the streets without any owner. I would have earned a lot of money by selling the dogs. To overcome the depression, one brings from his family life or the society, he needs a companion of his liking. It can be a pet animal. Perhaps this is the background of such a habit and, perhaps could fill the spiritual needs of people instead of being closer to human beings. Children meet their parents more closely usually on Christmas and Easter. Otherwise, no need. Norwegian youth has to consider very seriously for the fulfillment of their spiritual gap.

When Autumn Comes

It is October. The winds are blowing and giving a shrill music. The leaves on the tree are growing yellow. When I see the city of Trondheim from 13th floor of NTH main building, the whole city seems to be half green, half yellow. The life in the dead and ruined leaves is amazing. I like their color. Although the image of hope runs down while seeing them, but I could never miss the charm in Buddha's statues I saw in British museum. They also turn my, mode to solitude. In October at times, it is rain snow fall weather. When I saw the first snowfall here, I came out of my house and left myself alone like the leaves of autumn. I felt as if I was free from all the directions of earth. The snow, falling on my cheeks made the emotional man inside me, a little cloudy. When I see the real color of autumn leaves, I feel how close the nature is to the people of this country like a child close to his mother. But the Norwegians didn't take sorrows and winds as seriously as I took them. To see the real color of sorrow, the gloom inside me, I felt like volcanic eruption approaching slowly. The roads were covered with yellow leaves. The red lines on footpath are drawn for walkers and black lines for the cyclists. When. I walk around on those footpaths and, see the girl with blond hair and blue eyes, I find so many routes of beauty in my heart and want to do some mischief, but no Norwegian knows about the feelings of a bachelor and a foreigner. Can I throw the rainwater of rain from my umbrella on a pretty face and enjoy it, later of throwing water on every face as if they do on beaches? There is a special psychological condition of a person being in a foreign land, especially when he was in a country of white people where they have a feeling that people from tropical countries were frustrated about sex. They think we were not seriously involved in any feeling and sentiment. The women from Africa and their children were merry making freely. Perhaps they were not carrying any complex from their country. Looking at their lifestyle, I felt a man was happiest in the state of extreme actions and feelings. Some wanted to laugh at the heights of mountain peaks, some wanted to cry like a Dolby sound, and some wanted to fight like Mongols. The center of that expression and feeling is called, "Thought", which if somebody is en routing, then he is shaped into many angles. There was a man divided from the angles of depressions and ideals to the angles of search and creation; that was me who had strongly felt on the land of white people, Norway, that there were only two things with him; Himself and the Nature. I couldn't match my expectations in this country, which I took from my land. I couldn't fill the void of my spiritual life. At sunset, I usually used to walk to a very attractive graveyard outside the student town. There was a small church in front of the graveyard, there were flower plants, which were growing each day. The red flowers looked like a pinkish breast of a woman, the prettiest in the whole universe. I saw them very attractive along with each grave and felt as if it was a gift of fragrance from the living to the dead and, due to that fragrance, the person was alive even in the grave. The graveyard was green but was turning yellow due to autumn. Every Sunday, many men and women would come there and watered the flower plants, which made me feel that the separation of the dear ones had enlightened their souls. There were benches in this green graveyard placed for the visitors to sit and remember the departed souls. There were small and big trees at a distance of 10 meters. I passed through that silent graveyard very slowly and felt the yellow light of sunset penetrating in my soul. That was only once that I could see the lovely sunset because the sky used to be cloudy or snowing quite often. I had seen stars only once in two months of stay in Norway. The nights of Jamshoro and sea in Karachi were linked in my memories and if I forgot them that meant I forgot every truth.

A few days later, our course leader, Professor Bratteland invited all the students of our class to his house for dinner. By attending that party, I could know how Norwegians live in their homes and, how they welcome their guests. His home was built up in the hills from where I could see many other beautiful houses. Usually, the houses were built of wood partitioned by glasses and somewhere with walls. Some glasses were plain, and others were rough. It was snowing when our Taxi arrived there. There was snow all around the house hence it looked like twilight and was changing into the color of white duck. The professor in a green coat and green tie was standing at the door along with his wife and children. We entered and met their children too. There was one green light bar in his house at the entrance. Drawing room is at the right of entrance and staircase at the left, which led to the dining room, bedrooms, kitchen, and TV lounge. We were offered wine, beer and soft drink served by professor himself, a longish person whose head almost touched the roof of the bar. While standing into the bar, he was serving wine to everyone. I thought in the western families, wine before the dinner was served as a mark of tradition and the party is concluded with dance. One could sip wine during the meal also. Our hosts were very generous asking us to eat more and feel quite free. They were treating us as if we were their own children. After the meal was over, there was some American music playing on a CD player and, the famous song "Rock n Roll" was repeated many times. Many of us were also dancing. The professor also danced with his wife. Nobody among us could dance with proper footsteps but the professor and his wife did perfectly well. There were many dance schools in Norway and taking dance lessons is just a routine in this country so the people of any age could dance well. The professor was giving time to every group and was listening to everyone with interest. There were on display many pictures in his house. For example, there was the picture of a dangerous animal on the ground floor and in one picture professor was seen shaking hand with Mohammed Ali, the boxer. He is highly impressed by brave and hardworking people and had seen the life very closely. There were statues in his house, which he had collected from different parts of the world, he had spent much of his life in Sri Lanka, Japan, London and, in many parts of the United States. Besides he had spent some time in Rome and Barcelona. However, I couldn't see any picture from African countries. There were a series of pictures of his ancestors on the walls of the staircase, which he had preserved since the last seven hundred years. He said after tremendous efforts he could find the dates and names of his old community people. I felt that our professor was not an ordinary man. "Was there any special profession followed by your community?" I asked. "Before 1900, Norway couldn't do any extra ordinary thing on map of the world. Before that mostly the people were fishermen and ship traders hence my community also did same job." While seeing his library, I thought that the Norwegians were very fond of reading English literature. I found the books from Shakespeare, Kessler and, also Dostoevsky in his library, which showed that he had touched many corners of human history. There was an extra section of books in Norse, which I couldn't follow but I found the novel, "Hunger" by Knut Hamsun. This was the place I came to know that. Hamsun was a Norwegian. After few months of staying in Norway and after reading his books later, he became one of my favorite writers. The languages in Norway are called Norse, Neo Norse and, •Bokmal. All of them have almost the same pattern but they belong to different ages. Neo Norse is mostly a spoken language and Bokmal is the official language used for paperwork. I had expected Bratland's children wouldn't be living with him in his house but his two sons were living with him. They would be under 16 perhaps because after 16 years of age, the life usually starts at the university and the children are free to live alone. Mostly they prefer to live separate from their parents. The government till the age of 16 years pays the parents for the upbringing of the children. They pay almost 1000 kroner per child. At times they give money up to 18 years. I asked the professor: "Do your children live with you?" "Yes" he said, "I have two sons and one daughter, but my daughter was born mentally retarded therefore she lives in a school. We kept her in our house up to 7 years but later it was impossible to look after her in that condition." "Has she only speech problem or she is physically handicapped?" I asked him because I knew that there are 300 possible diseases in mentally retarded children caused most often by the wrong process of delivery. But during embryo life also, a child can become mentally handicapped. "She is very normal looking, but we had to support her at every step." The professor started to tell me. "She can neither walk by herself nor can eat or take a bath by herself. She never tells if she must go to the toilet. Once at the age of three, she started crying and kept crying for 3 months and we along with doctors couldn't find the cause of her pain. • We always wanted to keep her with us, but it was getting impossible. She therefore lives in an institute specially made for mentally retarded. This year, the government has passed a law that mentally retarded people should live with their parents so she might come to us." I was thinking no one is given by all aspects a complete life by nature and it never allows man to remain unaware of the things around. That's why the image of humanity and love were still alive, otherwise men would have killed each other. This was the very first Norwegian I felt who had a kind of innocent heart in him. "Was your wife related to you prior to your marriage?" I asked him because I knew that many children are born handicapped due to family diseases. "No, she belongs to another city, and I am not from the same!" At the end of this party, the professor opened the bar again and served Vodka, Scotch whisky and wine to the students. When we were leaving, his wife kept asking us to stay for another two hours, but we were thinking not to disturb their comfort sleep. But the fact is that the Norwegians don't sleep on weekends. Those nights are only for merrymaking in which they arrange parties, drink wine and dance. Members of every age group have their own ways of entertainment. Youngers like every youth of the world are inquisitive and boisterous. The night can't be termed as a weekend unless they don't break bottles of beer. The elder men are quiet, calm and serene by nature hence they arrange sober parties and entertain themselves.

Norway rejects European Union

The winter along with its joys and hardships was approaching in early October. The morning, of which we have our own concepts, was not the morning in this country. In Pakistan, morning is directly proportional to light. When light appears behind the curtains, we prepare to go to the office. Here morning shows its face when I sit in the class. I see its colors from the window which turn the shadow of Trondheim, the city built in the arms of hills. The people of blond hair and blue eyes work hard and don't care about weather. There are measures taken to face the tyranny of harsh weather. The sun rises at 830 in the morning (which I don't see around) and sets at 330. In December, it rises at 1030 in the morning and sets at 230 in the afternoon (should I say an afternoon or an evening I don't know!). Sometimes it is raining, sometimes it is snowing. Suddenly the sun comes out and people run out from their houses as Rwandans rush for food after waiting during a long period of hunger. A short time of sun and sunlight is nothing less than a heaven for these people. Now I could realize why they lie down nude on the beaches in summer. Their bodies have been yearning to absorb sunrays. The whole time, they wear strange type of clothes. It is a natural need of their body. To see others naked is not an awkward thing here. They don't see each other's naked bodies the way we stare at them like savages. In Scandinavian countries, cold is almost the same but Norway is situated on the coastal line of the North Sea, and its north is joined with Russia. As I have already said about thousand years ago, there was nothing but snow around these hills. It melted due to the increase in world temperature and people started to find jobs in the plenty of water. Today, this country is the second richest country of Europe because since 1981, they found plenty of oil. Therefore, they don't fear the misery of poverty in the next few years. At present the main political issue in Norway was about its joining the European Union. On 14th November 1994 Sweden decided to join EU through a referendum. Norway's common man lives in his own social sphere and is a rich person. He knows that as long as there is oil, hydropower, gas and fish, they don't need to join any Union. They think they don't need other people to invest money on their natural resources. It is a fact that Norway has passed a life of slavery for about 400 years and has passed through many hardships to reach this economic status. Small countries always feel that they should not be disturbed by major world powers. Norway's population is only 4.2 million hence their natural resources are quite sufficient to keep them living. The Government insures every citizen. Everybody has a personal number; people are given extra money to look after their children. Health and education is for everyone, free for the whole life. Everybody can get loan to carry on his education. The great thing is that all these laws are applicable to foreigners too. This is the reason many Indians, Pakistanis, and other Asian and African people try to get Norwegian nationality. Many students who have come here to do a two-year course are intentionally delaying their stay so that they could save some money. But in my opinion much greed and selfishness are paid adversely and bring unhappy results. Now a very strict policy has been adopted for political asylum seekers and for all those who try to marry here and get nationality in an easy way, not only in Norway but also in many other European countries.

In Norway, a referendum was held on 28th November 1994 to decide whether they will join EU or not. Earlier, polling was held in 1972 in which 57% of people said "no" to this question hence Norway didn't join it. Is that possible in our country also that the Government arranges a referendum before signing any kind of agreement with a foreign country in which national cause was linked. A democratic system prevails in this country. During this referendum, for the first time, people have some political awareness. Many processions came out in favor of joining EU and also many people came on the streets against it. People had the badges on their shirts telling YES or No about joining the EU. However, the Prime Minister said on TV that Norway will join EU. Many local and international agencies surveyed the situation and anticipated that 47% people will say YES, 37% will say NO and others will not respond. But the result came opposite to it. Almost 97% people responded to the question. 57% said NO, 37% said YES and the rest 3% didn't respond. Ultimately Norway didn't join European Union. People celebrated the event. Most of the favorable votes came from

Southern Norway where the capital Oslo is also located but, most of the people from North refused the offer of the government and said no. Central party, which is, called the party of farmers, peasants and workers won the battle and this rich but free country is not the member of the European Union, which ultimately is entering as a major power in the world economy and politics. One expert from London School of Economics said that Norway will have to join EU one day and they will have to hold referendum after one or two years later, otherwise there will be a considerable difference in their export and employment. Many investors had stopped their decisions during the referendum. The dollar had increased by half a kroner. On the other hand the secretary general of EU has said that it is the right of every citizen to decide his or her path of future. It is their democratic right. Many people said on TV that they will solve their problems by themselves, and the union can't solve their problems. Once the Norwegian foreign minister had served wine to his counterpart from Denmark and got signed those documents in which he allotted a land to Norway which is nowadays producing that oil. This should be kept in mind that this oil would be produced up to 1997 and until 2030. The graph of oil will not come down. Besides those European countries who were buying oil, gas and electricity from Norway at very good rates, might not prefer to buy it on the same terms and conditions. Therefore, Norway will have to extend its agreements with Japan and the United States, otherwise its trade would be affected. Norway is situated on the hills hence there is only 3% agriculture, that's why almost the food stuff is imported except potatoes which are really cheaper. According if they will have good relations with the neighboring countries, they could buy daily use items from them at cheaper rates. To import such items from far off lands would cost more transport charges and more fuel energy. Why am I interested to write this note of explanation? Because I think that a nation can't survive on political slogans. There is a strict ban on immigration in Norway due to the fear of growing population and control over their resources. This might not be a correct analysis but what I noted from the comments of different Norwegians is that they don't consider the people running from Bosnia, Kashmir, Iran and Palestine, etc. as political victims. Instead they think these so called victims can destroy another peaceful land. I have experienced a quite good number of events in this respect: One day some Iranian women met me in a shopping center and forwarded some pictures of women and children from some albums. "Are you against Khomeini?" one of them asked me. I looked in her face. Some past and some disputes regarding the religious sector of Khomeini were reflecting in my mind. His sector is very powerful in Pakistan. "All these children and women are affected by the cruelty of Khomeini." She said, pointing to the pictures available in the album. I went through the whole album and said, "Since how long have you been in Norway?" "Can you donate some honor for these people?" she said instead of replying to my question, "We will send that money to Iran." I didn't give a single Kroner to her and came back quietly. The wind was blowing and piercing in my ears. I had a different kind of feeling and could see a beggar in her appeal. It is a culture that many political victims display in some developed countries in the name of Human Rights. The lie hidden in their words and behavior of that woman was alarming. But I couldn't find the picture of Khanam Go gosh in those albums. Khanam Go gosh was a very pretty dancer and poetess of Iran. She was fired in the time of Khomeini in front of huge crowd just because she was a dancer. Her beautiful photos are still seen on the walls in many countries. The above event compelled me to think that we represent a culture of fake victims. We don't analyze our conduct hence are happy to be called victims. That false, selfish and stagnant culture is causing death to the humanity in such nations. We should learn the real meaning of love for our lands. To hang the hands before others and seeking political asylums are the last dreams of our people, which show their narrow cultural mindset. I felt much concern for my land when I came to Norway. Never had I felt such an intense feeling. The philosophy bestowed by Shah Latif for the humans is correct for all ages:

No time to be lasy in cold or warm, Darkness is coming, you may not find real path!

Winter Without Woman

I met Guri before the arrival of harsh winter and thick snowfall. She was from a village located in the south of Oslo and was studying at the department of psychology at the University of Dragvoll in Trondheim. She was married to a man called "Michael" from the East African country, Ghana. Her intimate and humanist nature can't be forgotten easily. She was on very good terms with an Indian family here in Trondheim. Since us Pakistanis have almost the same culture as the Indians and, we watch Indian movies very often because there is some similarity in Hindi and Urdu hence the Indians can become our good friends wherever we meet. We met Guri at some Indian family's house. She had a black child in her arms. "She is a Norwegian girl and lives in our neighborhood." The Indian lady Seema informed me. "But she seems to be a grownup woman". I said and Guri laughed full-throated. Guri is a cheerful tall woman. I never knew she had studied a lot of literature on politics and economics. She had an immense love for "Gandhi", the father of free India and its great leader. She was impressed by Gandhi's modesty, half clad in course clothes. It was December 1994, and I was expecting a baby in my house. The child was expected to be born between 15 and 25 December, which were the Christmas days. Several exhibitions were announced and had to be celebrated during these dates. Hence it was giving so much excitement to us for expecting a baby as being a foreigner. It was giving more excitement because it was our first child. Everyone was predicting that the baby would be born on the rant.

Christmas night (24th December) and it would be a gift of Christmas for us. Guri had a heavy baby in her arms, and she was remembering her pregnancy days when she saw my wife. Many times, she came to our house and talked about a lot of things. One day I asked her about Norway's 'No' to the European Union. "I think Norway has taken a good decision by refusing to join the Union". I was surprised to hear that as I was thinking that most of the highly educated people supported the idea of joining it. Guri was working on a subject, which is directly related with sentiments, and I heard a woman saying on TV that if Norway join the EU, it will hurt the freedom of women also. "Why do you think so?" I asked Guri. "Because we won't have our decisions to be made in Brussels". Brussels is a city in Belgium where the offices of European parliament are situated. They had recently given gold medal to the Bengali writer, Taslima Nasreen. "Yes, but your representative will be present there and you will be allowed to cost three votes. The other thing is that the union is formed to solve your problems and not to enhance them". "Norway is a very small country and it can't find a reasonable place in the union. Already a common man is victimized here at many levels and, I think by joining EU, his problem will increase." We discussed the situation for a long time. She thought they could have agreements with other countries except the European ones. For the export of oil, they already have some of them. She was of the thinking that Norway's culture was quite different from other European nations. "You can never find the 'solidarity' anywhere else in Europe like that of ourselves". She pronounced the word 'solidarity' in quite charming way and, I find no word like this in any of my country's languages. "The other major thing is that to my mind this organization is a very limited one and, it is not for the entire mankind. It is a block of bigger white people; they want to prove themselves superior to the whole world which I don't accept.'" Whatever be the truth, Guri didn't have strong arguments, but she had a strong will and confidence in her voice hence I didn't put any strong argument in front of her innocent face. The whole city was decorated due to welcome the Christmas. They had illuminated bulbs in the trees. Offices and houses were decorated in colorful lights. Green, red and blue lights along with white mercury bulbs were seen glittering through the windows as I walked by the roadside. Groups of dancers and singers had assembled as the squares of the city. There was hope and love in every body's eyes. Christmas was just after 15 days away as I went to take some documents from the reception at Moholt. The woman at the counter asked me; "Do you like Norway?" "Yes, when the weather is not gruesome". It is always snowing and raining every night hence the roads had become slippery. The biggest ward in the hospital is for orthopedic patients, people are normally quite healthy but usually go to a hospital when they slip while walking or cycling. "Why don't you like Norway weather?" the woman repeated the same query. "I like snow, but I don't like rain after snow hence I think there shouldn't be the snow even". "Yes, but there should be some snow before Christmas. There is no fun in Christmas without snow!" It was surprising. If there isn't snow, there is no fun in Christmas. Every year how much snow they must clean. Every year, these mountainous, scientific, bold sexually free and calm people, having so many desires in their hearts wait for the change of weather and nature as a farmer waits for rain to cultivate his new crop. "If there is snow, both earth and sky become white. There is light like the full moon in the sky and on earth too, hence Christmas is delightful if there is snow". She spoke. The nights are so long, and the days are brief of four hours. Snow is the source of light also. After seeing great desire in her eyes, I also started to wait for snow as I used to wait for rain in Sindh, but this year Christmas was dark in Trondheim.

Some days before Christmas, we had a baby boy in our house. While coming back from the hospital after a short stay with my wife, I saw a bag full of clothes, socks, bed covers, shirts, sweaters, caps, shoes etc. for the baby, hanging on the wall. It surprised me. With this, there was also a letter from Guri: "Little child, Welcome to this world! This world is very beautiful, but the fundamentalists have shaken it. You and your parents are so cute. The life you have got, you should live it as you wish and try to avoid the compromises, although at times you must do them". Guri and Jacob (her son) Merry Christmas. The letter also carried a paper presenting an abstract art drawn by her child. After reading this loving letter from a stranger in this foreign land, the tears rolled from my eyes. I came to know that Guri and Michael were separated due to some reasons. I was already disturbed after hearing this news and had thought that Guri is a very serious woman. Separation wouldn't be an ordinary thing for her as it was supposed to be for the other Norwegians. Separation in Norway gives a chance to the couple to decide within two years whether they were going to live together • or wanted divorce. A 'no' from any of the two after two years meant separation. Immediately I called her: "Guri, I want to see you". "I and Jacob are going for holidays tomorrow; you can come only tonight". "Yes, I will reach you within an hour". It was snowing that night, I looked through the window and felt as if I was trapped within the seven skies where there could only be snow like sky. It was rather unusual and painful to Norwegians that it was snowing before Christmas and the darkness on Christmas night. I left the house after an hour. The snow kissed my cheeks as if it curled fingers in my hair. Guri's house was a five minutes' walk away from my house, therefore there was no chance to be trapped in snow. As I entered her house, she said, "If you want to keep your shoes on. It's no problem". I didn't know in which world I was during the last three days; I had been walking to and from the hospital like a bus. I felt at home at that moment. When I looked at her face in her house, I felt as if I was a poor man and a real rich man had helped me but not in Pakistani way as if patronized in feudal house. "I feel easy without clothes". I spoke hurriedly. Guri became serious and I laughed later. I corrected my words. "I mean I will feel easy without shoes." There were bookshelves in the drawing room. I saw only Norwegian books in one of them but afterwards there were some books from Indian and Russian Writers as well. Two bulky volumes from a prominent contemporary writer from India, Vikram Seth were also there. I saw some albums on her writing table. I sat on the chair and started to see the albums. "Will you take tea or coffee?" Asked Guri. "I will take juice or some hard drink if you also accompany me". She brought a glass of juice for me. I was going through the albums. Oh my God! The nude photographs with nine months pregnancy. She had the delivery 10 days after the expected hour hence her stomach grew larger and became heavier. "Do you see the red sign on my stomach". Said Guri, woman had as heavy a stomach as mine!" Her child's weight at the time of delivery was 4.9 kg, and the normal weight of newborn is around 3 kg. I turned the pages of the album hurriedly. There were many beautiful photographs; the child was born, parties were arranged, many photos of the child, crying, laughing cutting the cake, mouths filled with cake. In some pictures Guri was seen feeding the baby, sometimes both the mother and father were catching the child after throwing him in the air. In summer, Guri looked completely naked, playing with the child on beach. I stopped at that page of the album and made breaks while talking. I felt Guri became serious with such kind of photos. She was really a cultural woman or knew how to behave with a man from the East. But no doubt she adored her dark hair child. She thought that it was the gift of her love to put her in wonderful memories for the whole life. She had dedicated her full bloom young age to her child. I completed the album and said, "We in our homes also use to keep the albums of marriages photos." She brought the album of her marriage from her old library, gave it to me and sat beside me on the sofa. A photograph showing her marriage with Michael was placed in the album. Guri's father is a priest. During the marriage, he was praying for the welfare of both the bride and the groom with his both hands on their heads. I liked that photograph very much. The second photo I liked was that in which both the Guri and Michael were kissing each other at wedding time in full view of the people. "We loved each other very much but now we are separated." "I know that, and I have some feeling for you". "But we won't quarrel with each other now". She spoke. "I was much disturbed after hearing that news and I thought you were not like a common Norwegian woman indifferent and carefree hence you must be going through emotional distress. I thought you were a very serious woman." She stood up from the sofa and left herself on a chair in front of me as if she had come after a lot of swimming. I felt she didn't like the word of my sympathy. Although I didn't mean to be sympathetic with her but perhaps my words conveyed sympathy. "What is the reason for separation?" I asked. "Perhaps Michael can give the answer correctly". She spoke. She was a woman close to nature's ways. She believed it was easy to converse with a woman instead of a man because while talking to a man, she had to be crafty. "Some people from developing countries in the first world often marry a woman just to get nationality there. After some time, felt convenient, they say goodbye to the wife!" I spoke my mind. She replied, "Michael was studying in Finland since last 4 years and knew Swedish and Finish, both the languages. It was no problem for him to settle there, so our relationship was purely based on love". After consuming a lot of time gossiping on different.

Her sensitive face spoke a lot. Michael was spending his nights with another girl in Trondheim and Guri couldn't bear it. "I guess a woman falls in love only once in her lifetime and she loves intensely." I said to her and felt my words consoled her. Later she started to talk about the rights of woman in Norway. She said there was a feminist organization in Norway, and she was its member. According to her, the Norwegian parliament before deciding had to seek the consent of that organization. "But." She continued, "I think it is not effective in real sense. It is correct that the women are not getting the same salaries as the men get in Norway like in many European countries. This body recommends that the payment for the work, a woman does at home should also be included in the budget of that country. It was very late in the evening; she offered me a bottle of beer. "This is to celebrate the birth of your child". She said. Her son separated since quite late from the mother was now crying, I thought I should say goodbye now. But to make a conclusion after a lot of discussion, we couldn't decide whether the couples of same sexes or opposite sexes prove better and durable friends. I mean is a woman better friend to a woman and a man best friend for a man keeping aside the natural sexual demand of both. Guri was of the view that she couldn't keep good friendship with men as she could make with women. I curled my fingers in her hair before leaving and said, "We don't celebrate Christmas, but I believe in the miraculous birth of Christ that He was born without any sexual interaction, hence merry Christmas!"

Snows of Gausdal

There are different ways of enjoying winter in Norway. Life is far away from the miseries of poverty, unemployment, terrorism, insecurity and lawlessness. Physical and social safety, entertainment, comfort, joys and, hard work along with good exercises are the benefits of life. A middle-class person like myself having seen the trauma of and an oppressive feudal culture could see that it was a different society. But anyway, I could never sweep away the complexes of the third world from my mind easily. Gausdal is one of the very famous hills in Norway, where many families come from Scandinavian countries to spend their winter vacation every year. That meant many people from Sweden, Denmark and Finland would also be seen here. Every year NORAD arranges a winter seminar from January 2 to January 8 here in Gausdal. That seminar is related to the issues of human rights. Gausdal is the place in district Lillehammer where in 1994 the last winter Olympics were held. I forgot about all the sorrows of my land when I saw Olympics on TV. There is a five-star hotel in Gausdal where every joy of a happy life can be seen in different colors. A ski training school is in front of the hotel and, a lift goes up into the hills from where people used to leave at their own, skiing and playing with their lives. There is one ballroom inside the hotel where many couples go for dancing after dinner, also one swimming pool where boys and girls use to swim in warm water. A disco club is there where mostly single boys and girls race after each other while taking beer and wine. Some other games like table tennis, chess, etc. are also available to all those interested in them. When I was coming with all the NORAD fellows in the bus, I saw the snow on trees as if live birds were sitting in. the queue after building their nests. Incidentally it was (10c) both in Trondheim and in Gausdal. Although normally in Gausdal, the temperature is below 20c. I saw a thick layer of ice on the river while traveling to Gausdal and thought how fast the weather changes in such a short time. In a moment, you find water flowing like air and the next moment, there is snow and ice. I used to think of River `Indus the moment I thought of any river. I felt concerned when I heard people saying that the development in human life and the concept of human rights came from the west. Thinking over it I felt myself to be hundreds of years back. My people and I live in a fool's paradise. While saying these words, I could never dress up in appropriate words the pain I felt. We had supper after arriving in Gausdal. To us, they handed over a full week's program in which I could find 4 days ski course and the topics to be discussed and speakers to give lectures in forthcoming seminar/conference. I was completely tired. There wasn't any person from an African country with me in the hotel room but a Pakistani to share with me. Therefore, I thought it would be fine to have the company of the person with similar habits when you are in travel. But the guy from Pakistan didn't like the naked artistic pictures on the walls of room. He said, "I can bear them for at least one week. Meanwhile I will avoid looking at them". The pictures were very expressive. Man and woman in love were shown in different pose in the pictures. Touching of sexual organs by both the sexes was shown in very artistic way that it gave an enthusiastic bloom to my soul. But my partner, a religious one expressed his anger over the pictures and expressed his sorrow for the Norwegian society and its art. That was perhaps the result of a heavy dose of religious education back in Pakistan. From the next day, a life with joviality started in full moon. In learning skiing, a learner is like a small kid trying to walk. Two sticks in the hands and two on the feet are tightened well and then, you have to run on snow. It is an art but on the first day, I fell at least 2025 times on the ground of snow and felt as if there was a change in every part of my structure. Back in the hostel, every part of my body was rattling like an African drum. Primarily it is terrible to stand even with the skis. You move your feet a little and you will fall. The trainers at the school were mostly farmers who earn wages from teaching skiing also. In Norway, the children learn to walk later, they learn to ski first, as this is their national game. The snow here is thicker and in larger quantity than in other Scandinavian countries as the country is hilly. There were a lot of snow peaks in Gausdal. People have their own cabins in these hills. They come here in winter and live for some time. In summer, the whole land becomes green which I could see in the picture cards available at the hotel reception. So I was talking about the first day of our ski course. Our teacher warmed us and then took us to a little steeper place. Then we started to fall, everyone at the same time on each other. Everyone in our group had a hug with almost each other on the thick and good quality snow. Once a Chinese guy and I fell in such a way that we couldn't untie our skis, which were tangled with our bodies. At least half of our bodies were buried in the snow. If I put my hand on the snow and tried to stand up, the hand sank down the snow and, I couldn't help myself. My legs along with skis were fixed within the center of Chinese guy's legs. At last, a man from Bangladesh untied that fixed chain of legs and we were freed. Once I drowned in the snow to the extent that only neck was to be seen. I thought I would be buried alive. Back to the room, there were aching voices from every part of my body. I couldn't recognize those voices, may be some African music would be like that. I felt someone broke my body and delivered all the parts of my fragmented body one by one in my hands. I looked at my stomach, it had almost sunk by an inch inside the belly. I was happy to see that miracle and decided to go for skiing every day. In the evening, the conference for human rights started. The speaker on the first day was an ex-managing director of NORAD and originally a Norwegian. He proudly said that he had spent about four months with Winston Churchill, the War days British Minister. With reference to human rights, content of his speech was that, in developing countries, the element of moral was high. But there were no intellectuals, philosophers or literary writers who could divide the subjects in specific and related topics hence, the basic concept of human rights was created in the west. He quoted some of the intellectuals from France, Britain and, Germany from whom I didn't know many. He also said that Muslims don't give any importance to their individuals respectively, instead they say that it was God who would do it. Besides he discussed the topics later taken for discussion regarding the conduct of donor and recipient agencies. He quoted one example from one country, which he didn't like to disclose that once they had reported about it to the government also, but high officials of the customs 'department didn't allow it without taking a commission (a bribe). Afterwards on some arguments, he told that the story was published in the country's newspapers as well. He expressed his dismay over the increasing population of developing countries. In this matter he admired a province, Kerala, an Indian province whose literacy had increased by 70%. In China also, a law was in vogue for at least 15 years, a married couple would have only one baby and not more but he didn't quote China's example. I discussed with him at the end about some controversial matters in his speech on the points, which I didn't agree. One that the basic concept of human rights came from the west. I told him about some of the writers from India, Bangladesh, China, Pakistan and, Sri Lanka who had made miraculous changes in the decaying culture of the third world countries. Moreover, the concept of human rights is linked with the feeling to support victims of the society, which can be established and encouraged by a group of some uneducated people too. He even denied knowing Robinder Nath Tagore of Bengal. The tradition of promoting a culture of self-supremacy has been witnessed in the executives of multinational NG0s. It was my observation both being in the North or South of the world. "You know about Taslima Nasreen very well but not the Tagore?" I said to him. "Yes, because Taslima Nasreen has written truth from the human rights point of view". He spoke. There was a Norwegian intellectual, Catherine, the girl who also supported me in this idea that those writers who could play with people's sentiments just to be popular in some other region; achieved undue fame in the world. European parliament had awarded a Gold Medal to Taslima Nasreen because she claimed that the Muslim extremists didn't allow a woman to wander in the streets of Bengal without Purdah (veil). This discussion could be extended after I read her books with references but what I saw in Norway was that many Bengali women living alone were studying there. If they were allowed to come all here, how could their movement be restricted in their own country? To some extent, their accusation might be correct in some backward localities as it happens in Pakistan as well. But what should a responsible writer do for his or her own nation? Should they blame the society for all the ills, or should they work for the betterment of their own people inside the country? This was a debatable question and I stored it in my soul. The perception differs from one land to another, and the example of Arundhati Roy came in my mind. She lived in India and raised the issues concerning to her people. I didn't discuss it with that Old Norwegian guy. Catherine was a young woman and, had come there from some department of NORAD. She was there with her boyfriend, Herald who was also an intelligent and a sensitive man. At the time of dinner, I exchanged views with the couple still unmarried. We were discussing about two different cultures of Pakistan and Norway. "You have been living together for four years then why aren't you married yet?" I asked Catherine. "Because Herald is still unemployed. When he will be employed then we would marry. We will also think later whether we are able to live together or not". I thought after living together for four years, it shouldn't leave any desire to marry. I very often think that in these countries people usually marry late, perhaps because they first want to establish sexual relationship and understanding. "For you, sexual understanding is of vital importance in friendship, but we don't care about that while marrying a girl". I told Herald. He didn't agree with me and said, "At least I don't take it very serious. One should enjoy sex both physically and mentally, but it is not the only criteria for friendship". He kept quiet for some time and looked at me. I don't know why abruptly he said, "But if my girlfriend has sex with other person, I will become jealous and I believe a man is by nature more jealous than a woman". "That's why marriages are usually broken here?" "I become very perturbed on that question". Said Herald, "I was only four when my mother left my father. But despite such broken marriages, no complex here is developed in the children. If someone thinks in long terms, then every society passes from mixing up with different cultures and that process is always in transition. If the separation and divorce in a couple doesn't affect people's economic and moral life, then that measure shouldn't be taken as negative aspect of that society. However, this issue will make some infrastructural changes and our society will face some changes in its shape which will create some other inferiorities". Herald was saying. I didn't refute him because I believe the status of man woman relationship stands in any society with the perception of its traditions and history. Leaving aside economic growth and, talking about socio cultural skeletons, I have felt that the natural love, which is created within, can't bow down before any custom. It is free to reside inside the human being, whatever culture the person belongs to and in whatever part of the world he is living in. That's what I have learned from a very short experience of life. Herald was always a student of music since his childhood. He had made experiments on Arabic and African music on his own instruments. Catherine had done her MSc in history and politics from Oslo and Trondheim. She was working with NORAD. Her subjects of interest were literature, politics, and women issues. The Knut Hamsun's novel: "Hunger" was read by her in single night the way I had done. She advised me to read another novel of Hamsun i.e., "Mysteries". She was the first person in Norway who gave me a list of Norwegian and Swedish writers' names to read their books. Hence, I liked her company. After many discussions with her, one thing surprised me. She claimed that the woman was physically more energetic than the man, but as she is treated a weaker sex in almost every society of the world, her physical structure couldn't develop like that of a man. But she denied having figures and said her mother had them. After dinner, the couples went dancing in ballroom and, I was enjoying music. Somebody came and told me that disco was open that day and the entrance was also free. Usually, the entry fee in Norwegian discos is 50 Kroner, but in Gausdal, all the days the entrance was free. I jumped from the ballroom, went to the disco and, started drinking beer. There was a court for dancing in the disco and some fixed chairs were around. Bar was there from where one could buy alcohol. Fact is that this was for the first time, I saw many foreigners in a disco court, dancing and enjoying. Girls from Philippines, China and other countries didn't drink, also the women from India, Nepal, and Bhutan etc. didn't drink. I saw them dancing with only their husbands. They would become conscious, the moment somebody touched their shoulder unintentionally. The women from Pakistan, Sri Lanka and Bangladesh would never be found dancing in this country. However, I had seen them dancing in London, perhaps hiding this act from their parents. I have seen people dancing in Bangkok, Singapore, Colombo, Dubai, Holland and, other European countries also but with the style people used to dance in Norway was marvelous. While dancing they don't feel hesitant in giving any kind of expression. People take girls in their arms, on shoulders, hug and kiss them on the lips and dance in different ways accompanying the music. What a gift youth is! I thought and, how great fun these people had in their youth. My heart quenches and desires to live with her for the rest of my life but maybe it was a feeling due to intoxication. So, before I keep on seeing them as a hungry owl, I decided to dance with someone. There was a Philippine girl who came from Oslo, I already met her in the dinning. I offered her to dance, she said Ok. We danced for some time, but she became tired in a very short while. I came back to have some more beer. Philippine girls don't drink beer, but boys do so. The Chinese girls and boys do drink. Rest of the time, I was drinking and saw enjoying people, dancing on very delightful music. Catherine and Herald also came but they were not feeling like dancing. The next day I enjoyed skiing. That was the first time that I made company with Pakistanis after coming to Norway. We used to be together almost all the time however they didn't attend the seminar and slept during that time. There were more than 20,000 Pakistanis living in Norway. Most of them live in Oslo and are workers, owners of departmental stores, wine shops and restaurants. I enjoyed good relations with some educated Pakistanis who live in Trondheim. On that day in Gausdal, news appeared in the paper about the presence of a terrorist mafia in Oslo. They were said to be Pakistanis. Police had investigated the case and found that those Pakistanis were threatening shopkeepers to give (Bhatta) tax and be free from their threats. I felt horrified hearing this news. Although the terrorism has a widespread mafia, there were some groups of same mafias in almost every country of the world. Despite that, I didn't want to hear the name of my country involved in such kind of news. Thanks god no one asked me about that in the hotel. The people from Pakistan staying in Gausdal were from different provinces, we used to relate the stories from each province to people of other province and enjoyed the jokes related to them. They were teasing me on the point that Sindh was very notorious for its homosexuality. I told them a joke: "There are a lot of stories about homosexuality in Sindh, and handsome boys live a life shying away from others. Most of them being loved by someone very seriously but were shy to disclose their sentiments. There was a story of a lover who had fallen in love with a boy, but the boy didn't like him. The man's name was 'Jaro Khan', who frequently used to see him. One day at a party, among friends 'Jaro Khan' asked the boy to go with him for a walk. The boy refused out rightly. 'Jaro Khan' became very angry with boy and said, 'you say "yes" to everyone but always cool (no warmth) for Jaro Khan'. On the last day, every country showed a cultural presentation in the ball room, which was called the international cultural evening. Students sang their folk songs, played their folk dances and, the evening was really looking like an international gathering. This year the countries that participated were China, India, Zambia, Uganda, Bangladesh, Sri Lanka, Nepal, Maldives, Pakistan, and Norway. From Pakistan, we were only five persons (all male) and were 'guessing as to what to do at the function? Many dances and songs were echoing in my mind, but they were impossible to perform without practice and rehearsal. I was thinking of performing such an item, 'which they could understand and enjoy. As every country was presenting its performance in its own language and, there was a communication gap. People would not understand our local and national language, I thought. They wouldn't understand our item at all. Hence, I thought Urdu would be understood by the Indians, Bengalis and Nepalese.

We performed a song and a dance, which is very popular in marriages sung by friends of groom and bride in Pakistan. Here it is:

Be happy, be happy and be happy!

Those who have golden rings in their hands,

Those who have green sticks in their hands,

Those who have red bride in their arms,

Those who drink green and red wine together,

Be happy, be happy and be happy!

All of my friends were dancing on tune of the song, and I joined them in the end. What a pleasant moment it was to sing your land's song in a foreign land. I remember many events regarding that song. Everybody was wearing his folk dress and in fact everybody was looking strange but original as if he was born like that.

The best performance was from Bangladesh who played a drama without dialogues, based only on actions. They showed an operation theater in which every action came without dialogue. I was thinking that after getting independence, Bangladesh had increased its literacy level and sent the people for training on merit basis and, not on influence basis as it is done most of the time in Pakistan. I used to sit with Pakistanis during dinner and lunch. Many rich people were seen from many parts of Scandinavia in the hotel. Many people were staying in their cabins but were taking food in the hotel. People who had the lunch and dinner with us were seen in the ballroom and disco. Not only were those who had the meal but those girls who served it seen in the disco afterwards with hardly covering their bodies with clothes. They were smoking and drinking freely. There are a lot of memories, which I took from Gausdal. Jokes, dances, games, ski, the memories covered with snow, a very short distance between earth and sky brought me closer to nature. For the whole period of my stay there, the stars and moon were lost. There was snow on earth and there were white clouds filled with vapors in the skies. Hence instead of night, it seemed that the universe was twinkling. It seemed as if the earth and sky were meeting each other at one point and kissing each other. It was last night at Gausdal and, I found myself in the arms of a Chinese girl. I was drunk. That beautiful girl also drank too much that night hence she lost her shyness; she had carried from her country. I was dancing with a girl from the largest country of the world in a distant land. She didn't know about my person, my background, and my land. I didn't know the same about her, even then we were dancing with passion. All the Chinese mostly keep away their women away from others. Chinese girls are usually very shy and modest in the eastern ways. They love only one person and try to live with him for the whole life. But my companion was like a female snake (I don't know her name even now), she put her arms around the neck and, I put mine around her chest and let her dance as if I was a conjurer in the court. Alas! If I could ask her name! Alas! If I could capture her youth in a painting. Now, I must cross the Great Wall of China to see her again.

The Biggest Ski Jump in Norway

We visited Lillehammer while returning to Trondheim and saw 120 meters ski jump, which was practiced in the 1994 winter Olympics. This is the town where the famous Norwegian writer, Sigrid Undset passed her last days. She wrote historical novels and won the Nobel Prize for literature in 1928. She was the second Norwegian after Knut Hamsun who won the Nobel Prize for literature. Undset was born in Denmark and lived in the United States for many years. She had written several novels, but I have read her novels of 11th century based on Norwegian history, i.e., the trilogy, 'Master of Hesteviken'. Apart from that, her marvelous work, is 'The Bridal Wreath' (Kristina Lavrandatter). After reading such novels, it seems that Norwegian kings were not of imperial mentality, but they respected the human sentiments. She described a lot of heroic characters of different periods. Her style of writing is very ironic. Scandinavian countries are little bit different in culture in comparison to other European countries. Hard winds and mountain peaks covered with snow give a look of wilderness. No poor man can survive here because nobody can sleep on footpath. If he does so, he will be high in skies the next morning! The challenging society where a woman divorces a man more than & man does it and a divorced woman is not derided in the society as in many South Asian countries. These women are fighting in life and are struggling to gain recognition and improve the society. That's why perhaps they keep funding in the developing countries for quality education. This is another way to recognize the importance of quality education in their own country. At times it is felt that by giving such type of training to the people of developing countries, they want to sell their technology to our underdeveloped areas where technology is needed most. We were discussing that point while returning to Trondheim in the coach. Someone informed that many technical experts were sitting idle now a days in Norway who don't have any project to work for. It might be correct, but it was also a fact that during these courses, Norway familiarized the people to know their country very closely. The courses were organized in such a way that everything from their technology, games, culture, and laws were introduced and explained to us. They are longing to be known in the world and are proud of their culture. People from tropical countries may or may not like their culture but it should be acknowledged that they have developed a fine communication system in this harsh and oppressive weather.

The discussion continued communication and teaching of theories. The bus was running through winding alleys in the hills with a fast speed. The Sloam River was seen fully covered with snow and was as if saying farewell to us while coming back to Trondheim. We saw the people skiing on the jumps of the hills, playing with their lives. I felt that a man can learn more in hard conditions and can therefore enjoy adventure afterwards. Some Indians also participated in the discussion and the topic moved towards the world's great influential persons. Question was that who was the best communicator among the Holy Prophet Mohammed (P.B.U.H), Christ, Buddha, Lenin, Marx, Einstein, Moses, etc. Lenin and Mark were born in recent centuries, therefore their influence on the society should be measured after a longer period although they had the modern scientific measures available. To make such a study, during that discussion, an Indian student, Rajeev narrated a joke about Lenin after begging pardon to all concerned: 'Lenin had to go to hell anyhow because he was against God. He was a good communicator hence when he arrived in hell; he started to preach people on his way. In the reaction, devil thought that now Lenin was turning his people away. After one month of Lenin's stay in hell, millions of people became communists. One day, the devil was tired of him. He called on God on a hotline:

"Hallo devil here!"

"Yes, what do you want to say?"

"This man from is out of my control, you give advice what to do?"

"Send him to me." God said with full confidence. The devil sent Lenin to heaven. After one month of a calm and comfortable life, Devil thought of asking God about Lenin.

"Hello, it is devil here. Can I speak to God?" The Devil spoke on the phone.

No reply came from the other side.

"Hello, it is devil here. Can I speak to God?" Again, there was no reply. He tried a lot, but no reply came. After some days he again tried because he thought that the high and mighty must be in trouble.

"Hello, devil here. Can I speak to God?"

"Hello" the voice came from the other side, "Don't call me God, and call me comrade!"

This way we passed our time having debates and jokes when approaching Trondheim. Everybody was expecting darkness in Trondheim. It was 8th of January and there was no snow and no daylight. After leaving behind the delightful nights of Gausdal, when we arrived in the darkness of Trondheim, we didn't like to go home.

A Landscape in Trondheim

Staying and living for six months in a foreign country, to be exact in Norway, the land to us was no more supposed to be a foreign land. It looked to be as our own land. Norway since situated along the coastal line of North Sea was charismatic, where every day looked to be a new day, if not due to any thing just because of its weather. Every day was a new day, and the weather of each day was different from the previous one. Sometimes it was not expected to be cold, people would come out without jacket and suddenly harsh wind with snow would hit the city. You look for an umbrella that you had left at home. Only then you would feel you were in a foreign land. There came a storm in North Sea during February. They had fastened the ships with tight ropes at the ports. In these months there is snow all around. At every alternate day, there is a snowfall. If you come along a hill, you will see the houses covered with snow at such a height that the snow and the house are not separately identified. But these are not just houses of sand at beaches. These are the real beauties of earth, which have created a different feeling for people to think. If a storm comes in this weather, then the cold wind will give a feeling as if one is swimming in extremely cold water and, when wind blows the snow from earth and hits at man's face, it really makes him miserable and helpless. At that moment he really needs sympathy. In those days I used to study for 12 hours a day. I used to go to library at 9 a.m. and came back at 9 p.m. The library was always kept open till nine in the night and, I felt comfortable while sitting and studying there. I am not fond of digging my face into books for 12 hours a day, but it was difficult to survive in NTH if you don't study well or if you haven't a sound background knowledge in your subject.

Once day I was coming home from the library at around nine. Suddenly the gale started to blow and snow began lashing my face. Blowing from the earth, the snowstorm started to blow on my ears. I had worn a cap covering the ears, a jacket, sweater, shirt and long johns. Yet all this and of course my own skin were unable to resist the stormy wind in this strange world. The snow was determined to seep into my underwear. The bus stop was far away, and the storm was coming face to face as I was approaching my house. My speed was slowed down in such a way that when I walked two steps, the wind pushed me one step back. In this way, the distance of half an hour walk was covered in full one hour. I remembered the warm summer of Karachi and, felt that I could face the temperature up to 45c while sweating but I can't face the stormy snow in 20c. I had no option but to survive from that stormy wind that night. Many fearsome thoughts were coming in my mind. I thought if I fall on earth, what would be the conduct of other walkers, perhaps nothing. Norwegians don't come to help unless they are asked in such a situation. So, if I fall on the ground and am still in the senses, then I can cry... help... help! A tired and hungry man covered with snow while coming to his house lost all the formulae from his mind which he remembered during the whole day, asked to himself 'Is the examination of weather was more rigorous than the pain of examination he had to appear for in the university?' The answer was ' There is still enough time to pass and there are many questions on your nerves. You have always sought challenges in life. Life has brought you at the top of land where you can't play with the flowing hair of your beloved under the shadow of a tall and thick tree!' I thought I was suddenly dropped on this land from a huge assembly of Sindhi poets where there was no poet who could talk about the beauty of his beloved. Today Norwegian music creates a feeling of boiled water. In fact, a man is intensely related in his thoughts with his geographical conditions. Nature pushes him close to reality. Travel to a new and new culture sometimes surprises the man and he is forced to think what he never expected to feel. The exams were over some days later and the union of foreign students planned to go for skiing on a hilltop around Trondheim called, Lyon. I also joined them. It was March and there was no tension of exams now and the bus we were in this time was crowded with many European students also. I didn't take my skis because I wanted to see some scenes with much ease and comfort. After many days I was planning to come out of the life cornered with books and leaving myself in the colors spread between sky and the earth. The group of foreign students stopped at Nidelva Bridge, which is located on the river Nidelva and took some pictures. Some of those pictures were pasted later at some public places in the city. It was commonly said that the whole Trondheim fjord was seen from the top of Lyon. The bus was not only crowded with Norad fellows which covers mostly Asia and African countries but also there were many students from Spain, Italy, Germany, Finland, Sweden and, Austria etc. hence the atmosphere was quite international. When arrived at Lyon, we were divided into different groups. This place lies between the open hills and there are many paths made for cross-country skiing and slaloming. I thought both the styles of skiing would endanger the life if people from Sindh start to play them. I was in the group who didn't like to ski on that day hence we were advised to go to top of the hill, which has always been very attractive to me. But before we started to climb, we had to leave all our stuff at some inn. When we arrived there, I saw a canteen and some rooms for accommodation. When I went to see the rooms, I was surprised to see how a tourist lived here. There were six beds erected one upon the other like the berths in a train. This was a very attractive place for people in summer; perhaps that's why they have made here a small tourist hotel. We left the stuff there and started to climb the hill. There was a German in our group who had arrived in Norway just a week ago. Another person was a Finish who knew about the hills of K2 in Pakistan and the other was an Italian. Three men were from Pakistan including myself.

Seeking the easy routes through snow, we were approaching towards hill and were passing through winding paths and, twists. Some steps onward we saw a landscape. I thought this country had made a place in my heart and while walking close to nature, I could overcome the grief of my sensitive and wounded soul, which I had borne in the past. The gale was totally different from the hills we have in Pakistan and, when it enters into the heart through the eyes, nose, ears, cheeks and, neck under the soul, it seems as if it has defeated the sorrow and has created a feeling of calmness. As we arrived close to the landscape, everyone cried with wonderment; "Oh!

Wonderful". On one side of the hills of snow, where young boys and girls were skiing and on the other side, the sea was in the blue through the fjord. We were in the middle. It seemed as if the Earth was not moving around the sun, but it was moving around us. We took some pictures as we stood there for a long time. I was jealous of the waves who have been there all the time and chasing one after the other. The waves were flowing together like birds. If the nations could unite like them, the situation today in Bosnia, Sudan, Rwanda, Palestine, Chechnya and Karachi would not be the same as it now prevailed but everybody sees the part of Earth from his own angle. The will power of only one man can't remove the utter cruelty from the world. I was standing on top of the hills and the soothing air of Norway was penetrating my soul. Then a painful feeling ran through me like a bullet train and the thoughts came running recalling the explosions and fires in the mosques and houses of Karachi. I mourned over the racist and fascist elements in my country. In a few moments, the water of the ocean thundered as if the blood of the innocent people and the drops of the blood touching my face. I prayed in my heart: "Oh nature! Give me enough strength so that I could make my land, green and could present it to the world. You have a rebellious attraction towards your beauty. There is always youthfulness in your love and in the blood of that youth, those dreams are also included which see the flag of peace shadowing the earth. Make those dreams, true!"

After praying, I threw a piece of snow in the water as people pray in churches, mosques and, temples. As some people have different faiths in many rivers in South Asia, I had faith in this part of North Sea that by the strength of that faith, one day I will see the peace on the earth. From there, we could see the high mountain very clearly and everybody thought of touching that hill hence we started to move towards it. As we proceeded further, the cold was increasing also because of the sun. In Norway, due to snow, the temperature usually moves higher because the normal temperature of the vapors coming from the snow is 520c and, the temperature on dry land is usually lower. When the coolness was increasing, one of the Pakistanis refused to go further but the Finish guy told him; "Now since it is spring, it will not be cold any further" The Pakistani guy laughed and said, "If this is spring then how will be the winter?" I think it was 10c at that place. Pakistani asked, "What is the difference between winter and spring here?" "The sun is there." The Finish replied pointing to the sun. We had been always longing to see sun from the month of November to February hence it was Ok if he distinguishes sun and clouds with spring and winter. After all, the Finish guy made us busy while talking about the weather and he took us to the top of mountain. We saw everything was looking like a grain of sand from that place. The city of Trondheim was looking like an island. At the same time, boys and girls were going down skiing. At that time, I became jealous of them because I had left my skis at my house. If I had them, I could go down skiing and would have enjoyed it, but I had to run and slip on the snow again!

Another Trip to Oslo

I had to leave for Oslo to get the visa for Britain. I called Catherine to see her while being in Oslo. She is 31 and working in NORAD. She met me in Gausdal with her boyfriend, Herald and, during many conferences, we had discussions on different topics relating to the cultures of North and South. During these days I went through those books, which she suggested me to read. I thought her taste in literature was very refined. NORAD in comparison with other international organizations is democratic in its political approach. It is running many projects in third world countries. Catherine had done her M.A in history and political science. It was the best time to talk with her about the international issues and cultural differences in Norway. "I want to discuss with you some issues." I asked her on telephone from Trondheim. "Yes, but you should tell what your subject of discussion will be?" I informed her of the date I was reaching Oslo and promised to talk about the topics before I could reach there. "Where are you planning to stay?" she asked me. "I am a member of international youth hostels and, can stay there." "If you like we can give you a small room in our house." I couldn't say anything about that because I am very shy person. A person takes many decisions based on his social background; he might be anywhere on the earth. I faxed her a day before leaving for Oslo the message in which I informed that we would talk about the following three topics freely and without any reservation:

1 Your Experience in NORAD.

2 Norway's "No" to European Union.

3 Freedom of Sex in Norwegian society.

I added some more words in the fax: "When you left Gausdal without informing me, I missed you a lot. To spend a pleasant evening with you, I would prefer to meet you on the beaches and disco, watching movies, wandering through any Norwegian fjord along with enough cans of Beer. Kiss your hands." When I finished my work in Oslo, I called on her. She asked me to reach her office. When I entered in her office, I found her with blond hair in dark blue suit working on computer. She looked very pretty. I put my right hand on hers and kissed it. "I don't like word perfect. Now I have to transfer this material on different pages and, I can't do that." She said and, I smiled without any meaning. Word perfect is an old version of making documents. She offered me her chair. Some colorful buildings were seen from the window of her office. The trees were bare due to the end of winter and sunshine was reflected through her blue eyes, inviting her to come out of heaters. "I have to work for another five minutes and then we will go." She spoke. "If we have to stay here for a longer period, I will prefer to put off my jacket." "Sure, Sure." I put off my jacket and put the CD on her pocket of cigarettes that I had brought for her from Trondheim. Catherine used to smoke heavily like many Norwegian girls. "This is for you, and I am putting it on the packet of cigarettes so that you may give up smoking and enjoy music." This cassette was of London's famous singer, "Genesis" for whom one of my friends from Mozambique keeps telling me that 'I like to hear Genesis during rains." "Thank you very much." said Catherine," but unfortunately I don't have the CD player and in fact I don't deserve any gift." "You will know gradually that you deserve much." She put CD in the purse and again started to give final shape to her work on computer. "Did you receive my fax?"

"Yes, do you come from the upper class in Pakistan or upper middle class?" she asked smilingly, "I guess you are from the upper class!" "I don't connect myself with any class but if you are asking from financial point of view, I am from upper middle class." I don't know why she asked that question. Since I had desired going to beaches, disco, etc. she therefore guessed me a rich man. After a while Herald called her. She told me that he is preparing dinner for us. Herald and Catherine were friends since childhood and, were living together for the last four years. I was disturbed for a while as I thought I might not find much privacy with Catherine in Herald's presence. I had a feeling that she also felt like that but didn't express it. When we were coming out, she said, "I have some literature to give you, but we will take it tomorrow from the office." "I will not be here tomorrow." "Oh. No! We expect you to spend the weekend with us. Right now, I will give you the report on human rights about Pakistan from 1990 to 1993." She came back and reopened the office. It was quite late; everybody had left the office. Catherine often did the over time. She was running through many rooms and found some papers from a file. Later she made a photocopy of those papers and gave it to me. All the time I was looking through her blond hair. I took many pictures of her hair up to the bosom but despite of my intense desire, I couldn't curl my fingers in them. There was a soaring sentiment passing through my throat. When we came out on the road, I felt there was no cold. The cold was swept away by her warm welcome. "Since how long are you working in Norad?" "Are you going to start discussing the topics which you have mentioned in your fax." She was very conscious of my questions. "Why are you interested in those topics?" "Because I live in Norway and, I believe that to live in any country, one should know the social structure of its society." I tried to satisfy her. She stared at my face with a smile. Her hairs were hanging on her breast like a waterfall.

"But I thought you are a journalist and, I have never been in touch with that community specially I can't rely on the journalism of developing countries because I don't know how they write and what is their approach?" I felt she was not true with her words at that time. "You can take me a journalist but, I live a bit closer to that profession. I am a prose writer. I may be a journalist in future." "What do you write?" "About the broken structures of different societies relating them with my society." We were waiting for a tram sitting on a bench of footpath. While sitting there, I felt as if I was giving an interview instead of taking the same. "How can I believe that whatever I say, you will not turn into a different shape and get it printed in any newspaper, which in return may create problem for Norway and also personally for myself." "There is no word, no currency and no action which can let anybody be trusted. Hence I can't be trusted unless you believe it yourself." I said and she smiled looking at me as if I spoke the truth. I think I was gaining confidence in her own will and not in my words. My words were in fact the reflection of her will. The tram arrived and we entered it. You don't have to show the ticket of tram in Oslo but suddenly a policeman can appear and check. Found guilty, you will be charged with 500 kroner. I talked about ticket, she didn't bother. "Why are you in need to appear in an interview to get the visa for Britain?" Asked Catherine. "Because they doubt my credentials, I may be a terrorist, thief, smuggler or a Muslim fundamentalist!" "It is bewildering law in your country that if you talk against religion, you will be hanged." In my country people are killed on the roads. Courts also kill those who are killed on the roads." "Why the people in your country are so lawless?" "It is very easy to criticize the people of third world if you are born in first world. But to be born in third world and seek a solution of the problems is not an easy task when you are forced to realize every step that this is a backward world, and you have to work for this nation." She felt sorry for putting such questions. "At times I don't think before I talk and talk in a hurry." She spoke. In the meantime, we reached near her flat. She pointed out to a building and said, "Beer is manufactured here." "Then we should go there first!" She laughed and asked with an amazing longing for me; are you really going back tomorrow?" "Doesn't make any difference if I live with you for a day or for three days?" "Yes, there is! But I can't force you to stay because you might have your own program." I thought I was in Norway for only three months from now on and couldn't live here for the whole life. If I could win over her company and her love, even then I had to go back anyhow. I could never convey these feelings to her. Herald entered the house just after a minute. Both led me to my room. Catherine took my bag and put it in my room. She gave me socks to wear. Their house is on the ground floor hence floor remains cold. The temperature on ground was between zero degree centigrade and 10 degrees centigrade, therefore floors are usually covered with carpets. If not carpeted, then you will have to wear the socks. In a moment, Catherine gave me a glass of red wine and said, "Welcome to our house!" Three of us softly collided the glasses and said, "Skal!" which meant cheers. Suddenly Catherine's cat came running and hugged her. She loved her with a passion. The cat was of black color and in Sindh to encounter a black cat meant a bad omen, but she was living with a black cat. "Will this cat always accompany us all the time, Catherine?" I asked. "If you feel uneasy then I can send it in some other room!" It was her kindness and as a host she had to show the manners but being a very formal man, I said, "No, it's Ok, let it be here!" However, I have never seen such a fearful and fat cat in my life. "Don't you like to keep pets in your houses?" Catherine asked me. In the meantime, Herald started to prepare the meal. Since I was the guest of Catherine hence Herald was working for her. "My grandfather had a cat but she used to spoil all the bed sheets and floors, therefore he left her far away from the house but surprisingly she always used to come back when ever left far away. "How far away from the house?" she inquired. "About three kilometers." They both heartily laughed. "There is a fact on record that a cat came back to her master from the United States to UK." "Really" I exclaimed, "But how?" "In the ship!" Catherine was sitting in front of me, and we were telling each other about our parents. One of her brothers was doing Ph.D. in computer science and lived in the same apartment on the upper floor. "Today my brother has invited his girlfriend at his house he is therefore busy otherwise I would like you to meet him." "Where from have you come to live in Norway." "My parents live in Lillehammer and, I use to meet them twice a year." I stayed for an hour in Lillehammer some days back. Two things come in my mind whenever I hear this town's name, one, Norway's great writer Sigrid Undset whose trilogy, "The bridal wreath" I was reading in the train while coming to Oslo and, the other, the 1994's winter Olympics which, I could see on TV. It is a small and a very beautiful town, that's why Sigrid Undset decided to pass her last days there." "Yes, I love that town." Said Catherine. "Because you were born there." "Perhaps, but I feel relaxed when I reach there." She spoke. "After how long you see your parents?" I remembered my travel from Karachi to Hyderabad, which is about 200 kilometers apart. Suddenly my mind went into the painful part, some years ago while traveling on the highway I was going to see my parents, an accident took place. I was driving the car at a very fast speed just to meet my parents at the earliest and, suddenly the car collided with a truck. It was a dreadful experience in which I barely escaped while my wife passed away. How costly it was to see the parents in my country, I thought. From that moment I felt as if life itself was a dream and I was talking in a dream hence I said, "Till the days my wife was alive, I used to see my parents every week, but she died after one year of our marriage. Later I rarely go there. My town is around 200 kilometers away from Karachi.", "Do you miss your parents?" "I miss my parents, friends, driving and, also the TV channels." "So, you have a car also." Then I talked to her about my routine in Karachi. Meanwhile Herald came with the meal and Catherine also helped him to serve it. On the dining table, Catherine talked about a leather factory running in Pakistan, which was throwing the wastewater and other poisonous wastages to a nearby ground of a village. As a result, the villagers were suffering from toxic waste, some agricultural land is also affected by it. Children use to swim in polluted water. "After many surveys, we could know as to why the owner of the factory was not removing the toxic water." Catherine was talking and talking, "Don't you have any care for your children's lives?" Later I came to know that this village was none other but the famous town, Qasoor. The landlord was also putting hurdles to start a project funded by World Bank, NORAD and, the Government of Netherlands. That landlord is the person who filed suit against the great Pakistan leader and, ex-Prime Minister Zulfiqar Ali Bhutto. Recently the same person got seat in National Assembly in Pakistan. "If a donor agency wants really to work for the betterment of human rights, it should have strong connections with the people together with governments. There are many NGOs in Pakistan, you should start making contacts with them and help promote some projects." I spoke. "They can work with Norwegian NGOs." said Catherine. Although it is her profession, but I felt she had some strong feeling for the development of such countries. We discussed on that topic for a long time and felt that despite the organized work of donor agencies, GDP of developing countries was not increasing while increase in population rate was almost the same. Except Indonesia, Malaysia and China, there were countries who themselves have controlled their population and increased the GDP too. When we had enough input of alcohol, Catherine started to talk about Herald's expertise in music, which she loved so much. I came to know that Herald was also a composer and, was employed. He had his own instruments including a large piano in his room. He played some songs of his own composition on cassette recorder. The feeling of sorrow was dominant in them but in spite of repeated requests by Catherine, and me he didn't play his music by himself. "We will not force you to play!" Catherine said to Herald. "I can't play music alone." He was saying that music was fine in group form. When other players were not available, it was difficult to have the total essence of music. Having such a conversation, I realized that there were some serious lovers of music in Norway. I told them about the background related with the famous song of Nusrat Fateh Ali Khan, "Mast, Mast." that every year, during a festival in Sindh males and females used to test their nerves by playing to music and dance in the courtyard of a saint, "Qalandar Shahbaz". Herald's hairs were exactly like that of a woman who dances in those festivals. Pointing to those hairs, I said, "The woman having such a rich hair drown in music and feel an exciting devotion in their insight. That music is the music of devotion. "They enjoyed my remarks and felt as if somebody had discovered their own inner self. After some time we left the house for a pub. Catherine being drunk seemed to be very happy and, her blue suit was matching fine on white skin. While walking, her smile was penetrating in my soul. I felt that she didn't want to keep Herald in any dark. She loved him and when Herald was talking about music, Catherine was looking at him with such a passion that anyone I could become jealous! I was feeling relaxed in their company, therefore said, "After a lot of time, I am feeling relaxed today." "That's only because of beer." Said Herald. "I usually drink beer." "He means that he is happy because of your company." Catherine said to Herald," he didn't feel so comfortable after meeting me because we both had come from different places." By saying this she went to the other corner and pushed herald close to me. I was feeling relaxed. I asked a question to myself. If it was only because of Catherine's presence, then me conscious wanted to avoid the presence of Herald. At the same time, I was jealous of their relation and, its truth. Except that if thought about Catherine in such a way, I didn't know why I didn't think about my wife and the newly born son, who were waiting for me in Trondheim? What for that interaction of thoughts was? What complexity of my situation my land had brought me to this end? We came inside the pub. "You like to have wine or beer?" Catherine asked me. "Beer!" "Beer!" said Herald too. "Oh! Men mostly drink beer." Catherine likes to drink wine instead of beer. I drink beer because it is cheaper. "Are you going to be a political leader in your country?" Catherine asked me. I couldn't answer. My mind reflected to the leaders of my country; feudal, tribal landlords, terrorists, smugglers, and Byron etc. I couldn't find any leader from upper middle class. "I don't have the art of speech. I can't express my views in any art better than writing and, I find no way for a writer to become a political leader." "Are you honest to say that?" said Catherine. She had an imagination about me little bit confusing and not clear. I don't think there is anything in my style, which shows that I wish to be a political leader, however there must be some love in my words and behavior for my nation. "I am always honest with you." I told her. Herald didn't like her question about being honest hence he criticized Catherine that she shouldn't ask in such a way. In a short time, we started to talk about free sex in Norwegian society. Before hearing me, they had a feeling that I was taking free sex in very bad meaning hence Catherine asked me, "First you tell me what the meaning of free sex to you is?" "That's what I wanted to ask you? I said, "But to me, free sex means, 'as you can ask anyone for dancing, you can ask any one for having sex too.'" "No moral of any society is related to the concept of freedom only and, it is not true that you can do sex with everyone in Norway, whether you have understanding with her or not!" She spoke continuously without any comma or full stop, "Foreigners take the meaning of free sex as if they can pull any woman to bed without any interaction." "But I have heard many women here, saying that they are proud of this culture and, they can do sex with anyone." "I think you can't generalize this idea everywhere in Norway." Herald said after a long pause," If there isn't any moral value in between, there is no meaning of mutual sex. To do sex with any one doesn't mean to be in love." "In fact, the part of world I come from, there, all the relations are broken and tightened with relation of sex although they don't agree with it, and hence such a sudden change of culture pushes us to think about it." I said, "Personally I believe sexual interaction is the name of mental relaxation and not of physical, especially in the end." "It has both the benefits." Herald said. You are very unlucky if you don't enjoy it physically." Catherine said. "Make me lucky then." I joked although I had a serious desire to make love with her. Both laughed. Everyone was quite for some time then as if a devil had passed from that place. After a while Catherine asked me about my ex-wife. "We lived together for four years before marriage and loved each other in those years with full zeal." I told her in short. "I don't think you can live in Pakistan without marriage?" Catherine asked a very intelligent question. "Yes, it is very difficult, we didn't live in the same house but sometimes stayed for one night. Despite of opposition from parents and, society, no one could break the chain of our love." Again quiet, both were looking in my face. I took the glass of beer and, called; "Skal." This time Herald started a new topic; "Some people are interested in homosexuality." "Do you enjoy it?" I asked him. "No, but one of my friends asked for it when he was in love with me. I thought we were very good friends but suddenly he desired to have sex with men, which I couldn't do."

"Actually, there is always possibility to have better friendship with the same sex but you can't completely enjoy it. That's why I have always looked for a female friend who can behave like males." By saying that I looked into the deep blue eyes of Catherine. I felt that Herald could feel what I meant when I said these words. I couldn't read any answer on the face of Catherine and, I went into rainy dreams. The time I spent in that pub that night created a lot of enthusiasm in me and, I started to feel that I will get a beloved once more in life who could make my dreams true, but life was pulling itself away from youth and, I could never stop the tide of time. Too much drink also creates a feeling of pathos and, calmness in me and, I felt as if my lips were sewed with thread. In such a free country why the routes of heart become sometimes so narrow finding no path? Although I have passed a life as a free man on the land of narrow paths! Then why not here? Why, since many days I was feeling that voyage of creation had lost its roads, all the characters were slipping from fingers and, I couldn't hold them properly. I ran after characters, and they were running away from me. Perhaps I could never hold them like no one could regain his youth. Next day while going back to Trondheim, I called Catherine from Oslo airport: "There are many feelings I couldn't express with you." "No need to say, I felt them." She spoke. I felt as if I had disclosed enough by saying only one sentence and had loved her while in the bed and she had seen the reality as if in a dream. "Why did you stay for only one day, it was a very short stay?" Said Catherine. "Catherine, I will meet you again. I have felt that I was here for a short time but anyway I will meet you again."

The Third World Love

If a man from third world is fallen in love with a woman of first world, what will he experience? I never knew about its future shocks, dangers and, rising feelings. Neither had I known Catherine was a bold and a straight woman. I had some guilt in some corner of my mind that I had hidden the fact of my married life from her. She called after some days. Since I was not at home, she left a message for me to call her when back at home. "Do you have some relations with the Norwegians?" "Yes, but very few!" I said her on phone. "And you meet them quite often." "Yes." "Daily or casually?" "Once a week." "I called on you, but you were not at your place. Where were you then?" "I was playing cards with friends." "It means I disturbed you." "No, not at all, we finished the game and only then I called on you." She usually speaks about the factors influencing the progress in developing countries, the miserable situation of nothing to do. Apart from this, the difference in nature, her commitments, busy life, good friendship, sexual relationships, her love with cat and, Herald.... Etc. "Do you think we have to talk something more? If yes what about?" "Yes, I think we have to talk about moon, sun, mountains, flowers, sea, birds, snow, the birds born on snow, the language and messages of birds, stars and, about the most important thing of the Universe; the earth." I told her speaking from telephone booth although I was feeling () 5c in my shoes. "Are all the people from Pakistan romantic and poetic like you?" "That depends on locale. In Sindh, every second man is a poet and, I am the first one because I am not a poet." The desire was penetrating my heart breaking all the routes. But the routes of love were very zigzag and hazardous like Norwegian roads. They were pushing me towards a puzzled, sad and tortuous path. I used to go for jogging in Trondheim wearing tracksuit and run for miles, get tired. I couldn't avoid the love with Catherine and couldn't control my sixth sense.

Perhaps she was advancing her hand only for fun. I didn't know how the Norwegian women were to react in such a situation. I had never met any young modern woman in present society at such a level. This country is very close to nature and, there wasn't any deep longing for true love which I suppose was not expected in near future. But there was one inclination for love in which I found devotion, excitement, beauty, and truth those were in my heart! I wrote a letter to her as if I drowned myself in the Atlantic Ocean. In that letter, I told how I wished to spend these final and loving moments in her company. In return she became very sentimental and drank a lot. She looked for me while she was drunk and, called me at my house in Trondheim. My wife told her she did not expect that I had not informed her about my married life. I think Catherine was broken in her heart and controlled her sentiments. That moment was very crucial for her because she couldn't express the call of heart at that stage. "Why didn't you tell me about that?" "So that I could have you. I was certain that if you would know about my wife and a child then you would never approach me. I spoke lie with you because I thought everything is fair in love and war. One day I had to tell you the truth. Now whatever I am, that is before you whether you like it or not!" I told her on phone from Trondheim. "I like your way of expression, but you are putting a knife in some one's back bone hence I have started to sensor my feelings." Catherine said. I had become mad about her. She told me that she had a lot of past experiences in past and, the results of such affairs being very painful. I was jealous of Herald who was living with her since last four years. He was sleeping with Catherine and must be kissing her. They used to drink together and, would be dancing together but love always to make a man hopeful and optimist. I was sure they loved each other but also desired that they should leave each other very soon! "You took liberty in a way that you should develop friendship with me and, I want to cut off this relation by taking care of someone else's liberty." One day Catherine said to me on telephone. "You want to cut off this relation because you don't have deep desire to meet me so that you can cross a sin." There was a long silence in reply. A rational woman in Norway had jolted my mind very quickly. I had started to count the rest of months there and, there was danger of separation before we met. That was an interaction of mixed views in my mind. On the other hand, my wife was highly disturbed due to this situation. She started to think that one day I would leave her and, she started to think of committing suicide! April had come and snow was melting slowly. The days were lengthening gradually. The sun now set at 930 p.m. At times I felt very comfortable when I absorbed the sunshine after a heavy rain. I felt as if after a lot of work, I had come to take rest in the cradle of spring. We desired that we should go out of Trondheim for some days but where? My face was giving a clear indication of my affection with Catherine, which I could never hide from my wife. Was it a crime? To think about this question and its background was very difficult but natural too. In an open society of Norway, the free love was quite understandable that at one time one could love only one person. Could some one count the days of youth, experience, philosophy and one heart for love? To justify his love any way, everybody formed his own argument because he was in love without any reason. This argument would make a teenager, very angry. Any argument was only good for those who had crossed such a feeling or for those who were diluting their feelings in one way or the other. Whatever man thinks, it is nature's way and, man does not make himself, the nature. One can put hurdles in the way of nature but for how long? For how long could he dampen his excited insight? My wife was sad at this situation and, was sometimes seen crying. I had been looking at her tears dumbly as a stone. At last, we decided to leave for Stockholm to come out of such a terrible inner war. We had been wandering in the museums, shopping centers and, in the ferries. I couldn't escape from the attraction of Catherine and, her memory. I felt as if I was looking everywhere for her.

The most beautiful thing in Stockholm was national gallery where I could see fascinating sculptures and paintings regarding the changing social and political structure in Europe. I delved into many of the pictures. First time in my life, I could see the painting which were speaking to me. I saw a gallery of paintings of still life and then, of dynamic life. Very strongly I felt that Sindhi society was also a stagnant society. I could never reject or avoid the pattern of dynamic life, which was shown in those pictures. I couldn't disclose any picture in words, but it was very clear that the society, which didn't change its habits in daily life and actions, would be termed as a static society where people would remain the same as they were in centuries past. Whenever you analyze yourself and introduce dynamism in your daily life; you would imagine yourself living in a dynamic society. There were many paintings showing reality very close to the original. Out of these were some of great heroes and, heroines including Agatha Christie and, Samson Agonist. There were two paintings showing rural and urban life of Europe. I liked both. In a painting of village life, the use of wine, hard work and economic deprivation were shown dominant. In the painting of city life, wine, freedom and influence of Industrial life was shown dominant but reflection of those paintings was so clear that I felt as if the people of those houses were speaking to me. We saw wide roads, people moving and the noise of traffic in Stockholm after many days hence felt some change inside us, but due to having a baby of 4 months, we were not allowed to enter any theater, film or club we used to walk in the evening time because mostly museums and shopping centers were closed in the evening. I like a special wine called, Stockholm and was Sipping in the TV room of a hotel and my wife Saeeda went outside to allow the cold breeze entering our soul. It was sunny walking day in Stockholm. We were walking quietly for a long time. There was nothing to talk, about and a very beautiful city shrouded in me. I keep quite when I think deeply! Suddenly we came across a church. "I love the church music." I said to Saeeda and we both went inside. We were listening to music for long time but came with empty hearts and reached at the hotel. At night, I wrote a letter to Catherine with full passion. I wrote: "I am not agreeing of Plato's idea that the existence of ideals was not of this world. When a human being sees the beauty and, truth for the first time in his life, that picture becomes ideal for him then he adds colors to his ideal gradually. As he learns from his observations and experiences, he develops his original picture with more colors. I think you are the updated shape of my developed ideal hence I wanted to pass a good time with my head on your shoulders. I wanted a train should pass through a Norwegian fjord and, the snow speaks to me like birds, the train moves faster than time and, I could speak to nature while hiding my face in your blond hair. Catherine, you come here anyhow in my life. Why are you so cruel? And why are you so sweet? Are you not aware of the cruel ways and, sweetness you possess?" And I don't remember what I wrote. I kept the letter on table and went for sleep. In the darkness of night, Saeeda awoke from the sleep and read the letter. She suffered from the hard feelings when she went through it. Those feelings can be named, jealousy, hate, pessimism, selfishness, anger, loneliness, sorrow and, destruction. She felt her life running out of her hands.

The anger and, the behavior of Eastern Woman dominated her, and she took the letter in her hands, tore it to the extent that even one piece of the torn letter should not remain on the earth. She threw it into the dustbin and dropped back into the bed. But she felt that even often destroying the letter, she was not at ease and, the pain of broken heart was all the same. I was asleep and, I didn't know what was happening to Saeeda that night. When I awoke in the morning, I saw there was no letter on the table. That was our last day in Stockholm. I was thinking all the time while coming back in the train that either my wife did a crime by tearing the letter or it was her right to do so. I found no answer from myself. I felt as if I was standing on a bridge pillared between two different societies!

From Denmark with love

One can't win against time; it runs fast and waits for nobody. It pushes youth away, sometimes it snatches the whole attraction of life as of beauty, of love, of truth, of nature, of beloved, of children, of clouds, of rain and of every reality. In that condition, one feels as if all the ways of expression were lost, future becomes dark, and death seems to be very close. One can't win against time; it has pushed me to leave Norway now. It is the country where I could breathe the sighs of freedom. Where I could think I was alive due to my own will and influenced only by the natural mountains, rivers, flowers, and fjords around me. Although I was influenced by my 30 years of complexes which I had brought from Pakistan, but again I could feel them parting away from my soul. By that feeling, I expected that a great change was coming in my physique, and I would be among the people of my own land and say 'Goodbye' to this land of midnight sun. Can I decide whether I had a good time or not? Whatever it may have been, I have seen the pure realities in the laws and social structure of this society, which translates the human instincts quite closely. I'm afraid the complexes, which I brought from Pakistan, will be buried in the liberal breast of this land. But Alas! I find no place where I could bury the memories of this land! I know they will strengthen my future dreams. I am sure they will strike me in each moment I will pass in future. The days I passed here will not come again, but the nights will be reopened when I will die every night in Pakistan! The schedule of courses offered in this university is very tight and disciplined. The courses are accompanied by many recreational and educational excursions. Mostly the students go to different cities of Norway from each course, but the excursion of our course was scheduled to three towns of Denmark along with two towns of Norway. Our course is related with the port and coastal engineering hence we had to go to Denmark for some technical reasons. The reasons are not necessary to be told here. This trip started in the second week of May when the whole Scandinavia starts to be green, the flowers bloom and smell, the people with cheerful faces come out of hash weather and enter in shinning sun. I felt as if some great power has decided to show them the heaven on earth so that the humans could continue in their belief in the existence of natural beauty. I was eager to enjoy the trip even when it hadn't started. Among my classmates were five Sri Lankans, one Indian, one Chinese, one from Peru, and one very conscious and sensitive man from Mozambique. I enjoyed the company of all my class fellows during the whole period of course and, many cultural affinities were built due to resemblance of traditions. The problems of developing countries are almost the same because every nation is dominated by the problems of middle class and people frequently talk about corruption, poverty, population hazard etc. There are many ideas one forms before he doesn't meet the people of that country and they prove wrong, a surprising experience he gets when he meets them. We left Trondheim on 7th May at 10 o'clock in the night. 8th May was the day when World War-II ended in Norway and also in some other European countries and that was its 50th anniversary year. I have already told that Germans occupied Norway from 1941 to 1945 hence this day of May was very important for this country. I never felt any pain in my bones about World War-II but there are some bells, which are ringing in my subconscious mind about explosions of Nagasaki and Hiroshima. I have also mourned on the mistake of Albert Einstein when he made the atom bomb because world was still suffering from the impending horror of atomic explosion, although the atomic energy has its own benefits. We walked to Oslo port from railway station. We were guided by the secretary of our department, Annie Marie Solberg who is also a very good artist. Pictures are depicted in the background. Her best picture is of a freak wave on the ocean. She is really a very or committed artist. When she was guiding us to Oslo port, I broke a traffic signal and was crossing the zebra crossing with red light, she said, "Don't you respect the red man?" "When there is no vehicle on both sides of road then I have seen many Norwegians crossing the road not uncaring of the law and I have also become habitual of doing so while living in Norway." I spoke. With this light conversation and jokes, we reached the port. There, we saw a naval ship of Britain and some naval soldiers from France, Canada, Russia, Belgium, and America were standing along with the ship. It was Freedom Day from Germany Nazis. Now they had come to celebrate the 50th anniversary of World War-II. It was not a big function but just they were going to salute some statue. This war had created much awareness among the people of Europe. There stood a statue of a man who was anchoring a ship by some rope. All the soldiers of above noted countries put some flowers before the statue and saluted it. Later music was played which created a feeling of victory. When we were listening to a briefing in the class, suddenly the director told the staff on mobile that everyone should remain quite for two minutes in memory of this event. We all stood up and kept quiet for two minutes. During the silence, the port engineers were looking very formal, one man was looking at his watch at every second. Annei Marie was smiling, my friend from Mozambique was thinking that many European countries had made their colonies in Africa and that they couldn't get rid of colonial rule, despite fighting and hard working. He however had a respect for the day. There are many islands around the port and the biggest island is 'Hovedaya' where one can go by ferry. People say that there are some ruins related with Christianity but what ruins they were not known to port officers. We were sailing in the boat. Norwegian king, Herald V had to go somewhere on that day that's why his ship was standing in the harbor. Queen's boat is separate which was anchored on the other bank of the harbor. There were two ferries to leave for Denmark, one for Copenhagen and, one for Hirtshals. The problems of environment are given more importance in developed countries, but bureaucracy everywhere is same. I could understand that when port officers told me about the construction of a berth (the place where ships are anchored) but the municipality of Oslo was not giving permission for its construction. There were some houses that had to be removed when the berth will be constructed. In Norway, even a small objection raised by a common man is given a due importance, although the Government could shift the houses and compensate their owners. What a difference is between that country and our country. In Karachi many people are occupying Government land illegally and then claim to hold it forever. Similarly, there are many illegally occupied villages and now the politicians put pressure on the villagers for their votes in election, with the promise that their lands will be legalized when they would become members of parliament. It is another story that no promise is ever fulfilled. People in Karachi are worried for their uncertain future and the unsheltered population but in Norway a common man stop the most important project of the country to be carried out against his will. Besides the port officers think that they don't have any lobby in the parliament and now that they want to make a lobby although realizing that making a lobby doesn't suit any technical man. Every country has its own shades of democracy. I always wonder that there is something on which a common man of Norway is proud of his parliament! After visiting Oslo port, we were wandering in the city because ferry had to leave at 7 o'clock in the evening and we were free from 3 o'clock. I had to meet some persons in the city, but I could find time to stroll for some minutes in the city also. I took beer in a pub and then wandered around different buildings and observed some peculiarities of the city. Although I didn't know the type of buildings, I was looking at without identifying them I entered a small but a building like five-star hotel. There was no signboard on it. There were some old Norwegians making chat outside it. Inside building, there were two counters in the front, on which was written, 'reception'. On the left of entrance there was a large space for bicycle parking. Since there was no sign of entertainment, I came out of the building. "Why is the name of hotel not written on this building?" I asked an old man. "This is the parliament of Norway!" The old man said, and they all laughed. "Very quiet parliament you have!" I said to them but when I told the same joke to professor Armsten who was going to Denmark along with us. He said, "The building is very small but there are 32 ministries in this cabinet." He was not sure of the numbers, but it is almost correct. "The other thing is that the ministers come here only to work and there is a hall inside it for procession hence they don't need any big building for that purpose." He said and I thought it is a big problem for a common man to enter the parliament building in Islamabad and, to reach the actual office of parliament, one must drive at least one kilometer. In the beginning of 1994, I remember a bomb was exploded in the parliament and for reconstruction of the building they had to spend around 20 million rupees. The guilty was never found. However, I couldn't see any soldier outside the parliament building in Oslo. Later when I was walking in the streets of Oslo, a middle-aged lean woman (I could call her a girl also) approached to me and said: "Do you like to have sex?" I was surprised when I heard such type of question. I anticipated an idea in my mind and said, "Yes!" "Do you have your own place or I have to arrange it." "No, I don't have any place but with whom I will do that? With you?" "Yes." "What is your age?" "30 years."

"But you seem to be more than 30 years!" "May be but I am 30 years." "It's Ok, how much money I have to pay?" "500 kroner" It's too much! I did not have the time and, I won't do the sex without any attraction, but I was feeling sorry that in Norway also I could find prostitutes like in Bangkok and Karachi. In Karachi there is poverty, unemployment, illiteracy and, terrorism hence many women are forced to prostitution. It was difficult to understand why in Oslo, girls go for prostitution when they can have free sex with their boyfriends, and they are paid unemployment allowance if they are unemployed. Well, to elongate the talk, I offered her the minimum cost, "50 Kroner." "No, it's impossible. I can never go with you in 50 kroner." She said and went away. I also walked some steps but stepped back again where she was standing. She smiled looking at me and perhaps was thinking that I was agreeing on 500 Kroner. "100 kroner." I said to her. "I can go with you for minimum 250 kroner and not less than that." "Why minimum 250 kroner." "Because I can't buy the packet of heroin in less than 250 kroner." The earth slipped from under my feet. Now I could not think as to why the face of this young girl was sunken and thin. "But heroin will kill you, do you know that?" "And I don't die yet!" There was in fact the reflection of an eastern prostitute in the style of her reply. "Why do you take heroin?" "Tell me do you want to go with me or not?" "100 kroner." Again, I wanted to elongate the talk. "I can't buy anything in 100 kroner!" She cried. "Then at last why do you take heroine?" I also cried, "Why don't you take whisky, beer, wine or any other intoxication?" "This is my personal problem." After all, at that time I was going to Denmark and ferry had to leave after two hours. In between. T had to see someone otherwise I could go with her and know the story of such a prostitute in Norway. Travel in a ferry is very exciting and enjoyable in North Sea and Baltic Sea. It has its own world and there is big city in this world. The ferry in which we were going to a Danish town, Hirtshals, has 11 floors. Out of them, every floor has its own arrangement for entertainment. There were pubs, swimming pool, disco, cabre dance, restaurants, casino, fauna swimming pool, shopping centers, a cinema and, a tax-free market in a single ferry. When we were going to Denmark, the sea was at one time quiet and at another time rough. Still the ferry was never rolling. We bought a bottle of whisky from duty free shop and were drinking it in a cabin. It is prohibited to eat or drink private items in a bar or restaurant. It is also prohibited to eat or drink in a cabin, but we were doing it. My friend Luis, who was from Mozambique, started to talk about communism and he was of a view that Marxian theory had not solved the problems of the entire mankind. Other countries like China and Cuba will also come out of its influence very soon. "If according to law, you can't speak against the basic principles of the state, what kind of democratic law it would be?" Luis said to our Chinese class fellow, Lin Weiqi. "It depends on the economic condition of the country." Lin wanted to emphasize over his point of view about communism, "If you don't have a single piece of bread in your stomach and the growth of population is destroying your country then there is no value of speech and thoughts." I recalled a Sindhi poem: "There is no sense of beauty without bread." This topic has become stale and as a conclusion, I have always thought that many human feelings have been under the influence of some theory for some time. "There is no theory other than communism which can survive in China." Said Lin, "That's why its leaders can't be disloyal to it." Luis is a very excited and emotional young man. He doesn't talk much but when he speaks, he does it in a decisive style. Anyhow I like his independent nature and with him. When the discussion couldn't come to any conclusion, he took the glass of whisky and said to everyone, "Friends, be happy and drink whisky, Skal!" Everybody collided the glasses and avoided discussing more. After some time, we all went to nightclub and danced for the whole night! I didn't remember anything what I did and what I spoke to anybody. When I opened my eyes in the morning, I found myself sleeping in the cabin. Ferry arrived Hirtshals in the morning. When we met at the reception, I was told the story of night in this way: "I was forcing a Portuguese girl to dance with me in the disco. While dancing in the court, I was dancing with that girl. She said nothing and went out of the court. I again asked her to dance with me and asked why she came back. She said that she wasn't dancing with me. I was extremely drunk and was thinking that she was dancing with me. I said to her that it is not fair and now she had to dance with me, but she refused. As a result, I said to her that I would complain to the security people that she had deceived me." After telling this story, everybody was cutting jokes with me. I was depressed and was disturbed in Hanstholm where we went by bus from Hirtshals. At the port of Hanstholm, many healthy sea gulls will be seen flying as if some birds were singing playfully over the grave of a true soul. Sea gull is my favorite bird. I know that it can't fly enough over the surface of sea, but it always tries to fly more. I like to share his sorrow with him but whenever I move to take a photograph, the bird flies away. Denmark is ' full of sea gulls, very healthy and shapely sea gulls flying over the blue, deep and transparent seawater. While traveling in the bus from Hirtshals to Hanstholm, we came across the vast areas of green land around there is a lot of green land around and many corps were also seen. Windmills were seen at 100 meters. We came to know it in Denmark where more than half of the electric power was produced from windmills! It is not surprising because the wind comes free of cost and is essential for our breathing taken full use of it. We saw the green and even surface of the earth after nine months' mountainous life of Norway. That's why I was feeling as if traveling through a land of very rich landlord in Sindh. There was for us another surprise to see in Denmark every car on every road was new. Roads were clean, smooth, and even. The harbor manager in Hanstholm told us that the government had given 6500 Danish kroner to everyone in Denmark for the protection of environment so that he should sell his old car and buy a new one! Hence it was illegal to have a secondhand car in Denmark. On the other hand, professor Arnsten told that in Norway the government was thinking differently but the environmentalists there say that more consumption of new cars will destroy the environment hence, it was better to maintain the old car. Chloro fluro carbon, which is used in the manufacturing of cars is destroying the ozone layer, hence it should be removed from the products of the country. It was the idea of Norwegian experts on environment. I thought, Oh! Sindh! Where are you? And where is world? How long and how much hard work you have to do for reaching the recent technology of the world! The city we went to see is a heaven on earth. If somebody asks me; where would I prefer to live in the world? I will say without any hesitation that, "Denmark". Lemvig is the name of that small town where when we breathed cold winds and observed flowers blowing here and there like a pendulum. It seemed as if the green land waited to welcome everyone there. Healthy and colorful cows were grazing on the flat green grass. I understood the strength of the words like calmness, peace and beauty. All the buildings were made of brown bricks and the roof was standing so that the people should not be bothered with snow. While wandering in the shopping center, we could see our faces mirrored in cemented floors of streets. We left our stuff at hotel and went for walking. My room partner was a Sri Lankan Muslim, "Thoufeeque" who loves nature. He had also lived in Russia like Luis from where he has been receiving letters of his minor friends. The department of children is his property, so wherever he sees the children, he makes friendship with them and after some time you see that he is playing games with them. Both of us thought that in the town of only 5000 people, we had climbed to the highest spot. A little far from that height, we saw a small artificial lake, around which cows were seen grazing. We started to walk and went far away. In Denmark, the height of 2025 meters is a big height. Somebody told us in the way that the highest hill in this town is that where we were approaching. I saw the hill and laughed. I remember, we climbed 500 meters high ski jump in Trondheim, and this small hill is called the highest hill in town. After all, Thoufeeque and I climbed the hill from where we saw Lemvig and the small artificial lake. I felt as if a small child after taking bath is sleeping in the arms of the mother. Water of lake was clean and colorful ducks were swimming in it. Those ducks didn't know as to which what part of the universe they were providing inspiration to a beauty lover and sending the echoes of beauty in his heart. We saw some children from the hill, Thoufeeque became curious; "Let us see what these children are doing." He said and we went down. A girl of 2022 years age was teaching different skills to the children for example how to cut the wood, how to make groups and cutting the wood in groups. All the children seemed to be of 1012 years of age. "What are you teaching to these children?" I asked the girl. "These are scouts." Thoufeeque became free with white children of a Scandinavian country. He took a cap from a child and put it on his own head and started to play different games with the children. The bearded man is a very different human being. He does not understand the language of children and yet they write letters to him. Those abstract letters, one day he displayed to me on which I found drawn different types of flowers, plants, trees and, other surprising drawings. "We want to have a picture with the children!" I said to the girl. All the children came closer, Thoufeeque picked a little girl, got her seated on his shoulders and put her hat on his own head while making the picture. "Why is this school very small?" I again asked from the girl.

"This is not a school, only children come here from scouting in the evening time." We took the address of the school and asked some names of the children. While coming back, the children were making faces to us and after wearing jackets, they came to say 'goodbye' to us. When we reached the hotel, we were completely tired and the next day we had to leave for another city of Denmark, Esbjerg. Thoufeeque liked to stay at the room, but I wanted the breeze of Lemvig to penetrate in my soul so that it could eternally live within me. There is only one beautiful church in the town. From the architectural point of view, this country has very beautiful churches. Pub is behind the church; rest of the town is very quiet and peaceful. One feels as if the whole town is built by God only for these small number of people. Why the people of these countries are so lucky, why there isn't any problem of population, terrorism, and lawlessness? What nerve and wisdom have they got which we cannot use and why can't we? I have been thinking over these facts since the last 9 months of stay outside my country. After 10 minutes I found either a beautiful girl or a couple passing from the road, I was walking or, I saw them like a hungry cat in their sexual urge! While walking in the streets of town, I went to a cold drink shop where a Danish girl was cleaning the shop. I inquired from her something about the town. "Is there any place for dancing?" I asked her while entering in the shop. "Yes, there behind the church." She told. "But today is Wednesday, there would be a very few people." "Do you like dancing?" "Sometimes I go there." "What about today?" "I am busy today." I bought a coke and started to drink it in her shop. A cold breeze of wind coming from the door entered in my soul passing through the ears. Sometimes a car of new model passed from there. I thought the people of this country must be liking the large crowds of people, but they don't give an ignorant look when they see any foreigner in their country. "I want to have some company in this elegant town." I said to that Danish doll. She didn't reply and I again sipped the coke. After a while she pointed out the golden ring in her hand and said, "See this, my finance is hanging in my hand, he has to come here and will pick me." I understood. It is only Norway where no girl would enter engagement. Norway is an indifferent country in this sense that nobody needs to be engaged or get married. People can have children without marriage, only the woman has to talk about the father of her child, and then they will check his blood and will give the social rights to couple. I guess in Denmark and Finland, it is not so. To be engaged and be married seems to be necessary for having children. I came out of the shop and walked for a long time and then had some beer with friends at the hotel. We were traveling through the western coast of Denmark. The whole country is plane and windy. On every kilometer, there are windmills, standing in queues. During traveling in the bus, green lands are to be seen. On the day we started our travel and left the mountainous life of Norway, we all felt as if we have landed on a plane earth like our own. Esbjerg is a big city. Summer had come in the recent days around the center of the city, which was well crowded. There were pubs around every corner of Centrum (center of the city) and people were sitting on the chairs drinking beer. A big statue of a hero was standing exact in the center. Here in Norway and, Denmark and, maybe in Finland and Sweden also, it is a tradition to put a statue of a warrior hero in the middle of the city. The people of Denmark are very frank and handsome. Norwegians are tall and pinkish in color, but the Danish people are average in height and white in color. If we don't examine closely on their structure, we will find no difference in the people of whole Scandinavia because mostly all people have blond hair and blue eyes. From the center of Esbjerg, every street is opening to a shopping center and, to walk in those streets is really an end of a long journey and, the heart doesn't like to leave these streets. The heart says to speak with Catherine. I know that she had recently come back from Tanzania, and she would be excited about her journey. I called her: "How was your journey?" "Very nice, the people are so beautiful and truthful. I have gone there after 22 years and, stayed in the same hotel where I had stayed 22 years ago. There were many people who couldn't expect me that I will ever meet them." "It seems that you have enjoyed a lot from your stay." "Oh! Sure and, how are you'?" "Me, I am talking from the heaven on earth this time." "Are you in Denmark?" she said, "In which city?" "Esbjerg. The time will snatch these moments and, this place but, I will never forget about them." I said to her talking from the phone in the Centrum of Esbjerg, "I will stay till the weekend in Oslo while going back and, that one day I want to spend with you." She made unrealistic excuses like," I usually work a lot on Fridays and, get tired. I don't know whether I will see you or not. After all you should ring me, and I will decide later." I came outside the telephone booth and, entered in a souvenir shop where I bought a souvenir in which a boat was seen approaching in the ocean of snow and, written on the boat was Denmark. The cold breeze was making inroads in my heart during the whole evening in Esbjerg. There were beautiful people, colorful nature, freedom, carefree woman, sexual attraction etc. Where was I, I suddenly thought. Wherever I was, a middle-class person puts himself in different chains, but different measures of beauty are built in his soul. The whole downside and upside of the earth is seen from the floor of middle class and, any time one can push himself from the emotional cover of his surroundings. Sometimes you can never escape from those emotions. Shall I always live with the middle-class complexes? The complexes which always stimulate the person 'to have towards a nation of ethnic, religious and cumulative difference. If there wouldn't be any complex of the land, I would never recall my earth by living 10 months away from it. I called Catherine again: "I went to pass a few good moments during my journey with you." "But I won't disturb your family life." "And are you happy to disturb my inner life?" "No!" she said slowly and lovingly." I don't know why you are so naughty. You always keep trying." "Because I am sure about my feeling." I said," I want to buy some wine for you from Denmark. What would you like?" "No. No. Nothing, please, nothing." Now slowly she was agreeing with me. I said goodbye to her and thought one should employ some tricks to convince the woman. For a moment I came out of my emotional state and started to think about those tricks. By going closer to Catherine, I have felt that in the world, some women are still the same as they should be. They wouldn't consciously keep themselves away from the men to fasten them. The night in Esbjerg was very charming. There are some fine discos and pubs here. There are also good fauna swimming pools where men and women take bath together. We went to a small pub in the night where they had made a small dancing court also. We were drinking. After seeing a different color and, style of Danish people, we desired to go closer to them and talk to them. There was a young couple sitting just in front of us in the pub. The girl seemed to be heavily drunk and, was in a jolly mood. In our group, a young Indian guy, Devdata Bose went to sit with her without any hesitation. Bose is 23, the youngest in our group. However, the others are around 30 and 35 years of age. Many mischievous acts of Bose are funny and sometimes very typical and annoying to some. Sometimes all of us get bored from him that's why nobody was ready to stay with him in the hotel during the trip. He was very unlucky in case of girls. He asked many girls to dance with him in Gausdal but was refused flatly and, he was sorry all the time then he started to dance with the wives of his friends. Thanks God my wife was in Trondheim at the time. Later he used to tell the wrong stories to his partner whosoever was in his room. Despite that he is very good at heart and whatever he says, it comes from his heart. On that night in Esbjerg, he followed a girl and was talking to her several times. For quite a lot of time, the girl was seen with him. Later he told me that the father of this girl had divorced her mother and, she was now living with the mother. Her father has married again hence she was very sad. I believed the story was true but didn't believe the sorrow of the girl because to divorce and many again is not very uncommon in this society. There was the same young couple sitting on the same sofa where Boss and the girl were siting. The intoxicated girl called all of us when she saw that we were all foreigners. We were 34 people. We came to know that it was her first day in any disco. She had crossed the limit of 18 years that day. She had started taking beer also from the same day. In Norway, the underage limit is 16. Before that one can't drink and can't have sex either. In Denmark the age limit is 18. After that age the young people can live alone and leave their parents. The government is bound to bear their expenses. That girl was 18 years old on that day. Thus, we can say that Norway had developed an idea that they were more modem, free and more democratic in comparison to even the other Scandinavian countries. It was also the reason that the Norwegians don't mingle easily with the foreigners. The girl's name was Susanne and, she was talking a lot. All she was talking was not so serious to talk about. For example, how to dance, what countries should be seen, what foods or what drinks she liked... etc. Her boyfriend was taking care of her instead of being jealous and was repeatedly saying: "She is drunk today." "I am not that much drunk but, I am by nature very social." The girl said and hugged Thoufeeque, "How do you think, friend." My Muslim friend was disturbed and depressed for a short time. He had lived in Russia for four years and had never touched any women yet. He was not even married 'yet so when a very pretty and, tender girl put her hands on his shoulders, he became shy. "You are shirking your boyfriend." Thoufeeque said. "Forget about him." Said Susanne:" I met him just today and, he pushed me to come over here." I was thinking to dance with her because it is a fun to dance when you are drunk. Hence, I offered her to dance. She danced with me for a while. Then I came to hotel and, slept well.

The Unseen Moon of Oslo

Next day being a part of educational tour, we went to see a lighthouse, which is built at a great height, and the sea is clearly seen from its top. While along with the row of flowers, I saw the frothy waves rolling with the sand. Many undefined feelings arose in my heart. Why the soul always cries to drown oneself into the sea and the body wants to be alive along with the soul which perhaps is not possible. This experience of the sea relates with the universe of one's own inner world, which is to be discovered gradually, and travels, from unconscious to the conscious. We were coming to Hirtshals across another road by bus from where we had to catch the ferry for the Norwegian city, Kristiansand. We went to see the highest place of Denmark through that way. That place was highest according to the available drawing of Denmark. What a beautiful place it was! I was surprised that how beautiful the scene was looking from that height. A lake was seen in between the colors, flowers, and small buildings like a picture of Van Gogh. The scene remained intact. in my eyes up to Hirtshals. We did the last shopping of Denmark where Anne Marie brought the sweet wine, 'Martini', which is liked by almost everybody in our group. She gave the wine in very small glasses. We felt from her and the behavior of Professor Arnsten that this was a very friendly and a free tour. I remember when Anne Marie was saying goodbye to us, she said, "Mind your behavior please." which is in fact an elderly advice. Here in Scandinavia, many people come from the third world keeping the ambition to enjoy free sex and, they believe Scandinavians so ready to do sex hence they lose their control when they see women almost nude on roads. The ferry from Hirtshals to Kristiansand was rolling. It was a small, narrow, and old ferry on which there were no signs of disco, bar, and any Portuguese girl around. There was only a small duty-free shop from where I bought a bottle of wine for Catherine and my favorite whisky, Chivas Regal for myself. We were tired and the ferry didn't allow us to sleep well. When we were doing breakfast in a small restaurant in Kristiansand, it was felt as if the restaurant was rolling. One person dropped his teacup as he was taking it from the counter. Kristiansand is a very good route to enter Norway through coastal line because it is located close to European ports. Many ferries go to Denmark, England, and Germany from this port. However, there is a traffic system from Oslo and, Stavanger also but this port is busier for international traffic. We saw life in this city. Many colorful faces, Church, and the sun just in front of the fjord. We felt we had entered in a city humming with life. Luis, who had been always angry at the rainy weather of Trondheim, enjoyed the sun in Kristiansand. He said, "This is also a city of Norway, but her life is a bit costlier." Boss was eating ice cream in front of a shop, pointing to him Luis said, "Look foreigners like to enjoy the life here." I called Catherine: "You should not be so strict in your decision. I am coming to Oslo today and, want to see you." "I won't come closer to you because it will affect the emotional life of your wife." She spoke. "If we meet, it doesn't mean that we will come closer. We will meet as friends." "No. That is too difficult. If we meet, we will certainly come closer." "What do you mean by coming closer?" I asked. "Meaning" she started to say something but stopped again and perhaps changed her words and said," I mean you are very dangerous man." I had already bought a bottle of wine for her hence said, "How can I give you the bottle of wine, which I have bought for you from Denmark?" "Oh! Why did you buy it? You are a very difficult man." Now she understood that she could escape from her decision easily which she always wanted. "Ok. At what time you will arrive in Oslo?" I told her the time and she save me the name of the restaurant where we had to meet. I was talking with Luis in the train about the freedom of human expression. He didn't agree with the ideal that there was any provision for the freedom of expression in any law of any state. "If we can't criticize any person who is spoiling this world then what kind of freedom it is?" he said. I started to talk about his four years' stay in Russia. When I told him that I have studied thoroughly the books and life of many Russian writers like Dostoevsky, Tolstoy, Chekhov, Gorki and, Mayakovski and, I think there would be a peaceful life in Russia in some days. Later he said, "Do you frame your opinion from books only?" I saw his face and said nothing. "Every society is an unbalanced society in this world. Everybody will get money according to quota system when he will work more than his energy. There was poverty in some parts of Russia in the days of communism. People wanted to kill each other but couldn't do anything because of the pressure of law and, now the same fire is burning." The wife of Luis is a beautiful

Russian woman. She still travels on Russian passport although she lives with her husband in Mozambique. She has kept her passport so that her parents can get the fixed quota of amenities from the government on her passport. That's why both the husband and wife face a lot of trouble if they want to stay in a country for a longer period than three months. I really love Luis and could guess the trouble he would be facing in Mozambique while living with a beautiful white Russian wife. World Bank had declared Mozambique as the poorest country of the world in 1995. According to him, everyone expects more money if he sees any white person on the road. Our official excursion ended when we arrived in Oslo. When I entered in the restaurant; Catherine had told me, I saw her wearing a brown sweater. There was a cup of coffee and, a cake in front of her and, she was reading paper. "Welcome back to Norway." She said to me. I took her hand and, kissed it. "I was going home now. If you hadn't come in a few minutes, I would have gone." She spoke. I saw her with a meaningful smile. Although I was very much tired but there was a feeling of drunkenness on seeing her. I couldn't sleep in the ferry for even three hours and the head was whirling in Kristiansand due to that travel. Again, I had a tiresome discussion with Luis in 45 hours train journey. I was totally out of romantic mood. When my mind settled after a few moments, I felt as if she was not the same Catherine who had been the center of my dreams for two months. She was not the same whose love had penetrated as a flood in the dry land of my soul. I couldn't see those attractive eyes on her face, which I had seen last time at her house while drinking wine. "I am feeling strange with you." I said," We have been talking on telephone since many days, but I feel as if you are some other woman on phone and today you are looking something else." "Look! You have opened this story and, you have been running after me taking the same flag of interest. You are active in our relation and, I am passive." She said with a feeling insecurity and insult, "and now you are feeling strange with me." "I mean the difference of two personalities. Till today I couldn't find the point where your and my feelings are going to match." I said, "The other thing is that I never have forced you. I have always told you that I want to express my feelings and you have allowed me." She admitted. "What do you want from me?" She wanted to be open. "I can't keep it in one circle but, it is my desire to travel with you in train which must be going through the Norwegian fjords. There should be a river on one side and, the glaciers on the other. And I must be reclining on your shoulders during the journey. I must be kissing you all the time. Sometimes I want to see you naked!" "But you will not like me." "It will be your luck and, then I can leave you for the whole life." I took a glass of beer from the counter. "I feel as if you have never been refused by any woman and, you have never been defeated anywhere hence you think yourself, a winner. Perhaps that's why you are sure that I will be pulled towards you. You have superiority complex." "Love is a mirror of very tender feelings. There is no question of inferiority or superiority complex in it." I said to a Norwegian girl Catherine, who had blue eyes and blond hair, "But it is true that when you saw me with loving eyes in Gausdal, I felt that I can come near you and can spend some unforgettable moments with you in Norway. Tell me, didn't you see me with inviting eyes in Gausdal? Why did you see like that? And now how can you claim that you have no interest in me when you are analyzing me. That only shows that..." "That I love you." She cut my sentence, "Do you want to say that? But truth is that when I saw you first time, I felt sexual attraction in you." "Without any feelings?" I asked her to look in her eyes. "That depends on different nerves and figure of human body. Some instincts are only reserved for sex. They have nothing to do with feelings." I was surprised hearing her ideas. I belonged to a land of mysticism and was eager to see the developed Sindh. The difference between me and her society was that of a vacuum in souls. The laws and means of her society begin from the body and end at soul. However, in our society when someone falls in love, he begins from the body but ends at the soul. Catherine was a woman who attracted me sexually and I was pulled towards her. Throughout her life, she had boy friends from Asia to South America. I don't know why she considered my sentiment as puzzling. I couldn't properly dress up my feeling that evening in Oslo. "Let's do that today." I invited her to stay with me. "But now, it is very puzzling. Your domestic life is disturbed because of our relation and, that I never wanted." I stared at her and, said nothing. "Look!" she said with a request. "If I go home early today, will you be disturbed?" "Not too much but I have dreamed to spend the whole day and night with you in Oslo."

"I am very tired although it is very pleasant to be with you. You are very romantic. I like your poetic feelings." I felt a scar on my soul. "Where will you stay today?" she asked me. "I want to stay in a hotel. Let's leave this stuff there and, have some beer." "Let's go." I started to curl my fingers in her hair when we sat in the taxi. She stopped and said, "Don't do that." "Why?" "Because I don't want!" We entered in a hotel and, she spoke on the counter in Norse. I showed my passport and filled a form. "Do you want a smoking room or no smoking?" the girl asked me. I looked at Catherine because I never knew whether she would stay with me or will go to her house. She glanced at me, which meant nothing. Although I don't smoke but, I said "Smoking." "I will not stay with you." Said Catherine. The girl at the reception was smiling seeing a stupid Asian with a Norwegian girl. "But I do smoke sometimes." We proceeded towards lift. I came back for a moment and said to the reception girl, "Your smile is very meaningful." She and, Catherine both laughed and, I liked their laugh. I saw Catherine from feet to head with greedy eyes and thought if she is not living with me today then why has she worn an attractive sweater. And why the skin of her breast is seen through her clothes? I entered in the room, she gave the stuff to me and stood at the door like an Asian girl. "Are you feeling insecure with me?" I asked. "No. Not at all." "Then why don't you come inside. Let's have some beer here and, then we will go for a walk." "No. I want to go outside." "Ok. Let me wash my face." "Oh! Sure." We went to a pub when we came outside the hotel. I didn't know about the roads of Oslo hence I was simply following her. If she wanted, she could kidnap or rob me but in Norway, I never felt insecure. In this country, nothing can be lost other than the heart. Nothing could be stolen other than the belief and no one can push you for doing anything against your will unless you invite him. She was trembling while walking on the road as she had worn sea through clothes. "It's very cold today." I offered her my jacket, but she refused to take it. When icy cold breeze passed by, I put my jacket on her shoulders and said, "I can't understand why you are still unfriendly with me?" She wore the jacket, and I was left with only one sweater. I took the advantage of that situation and said giving my hand to her," Why don't you put your hand in mine and warm it?" She took my hand, pressed it and left it. "Just for a moment only?" I asked. "I am satisfied from that." "You are satisfied within a time of microsecond only." She laughed. We entered in a pub now. We were talking about many small things. I sat on a sofa. It was 11.0 0' clock in the night. We both were very much tired but• remained together because we wanted to be. She put her purse between her and me on the sofa of pub. I felt it was her deliberate action. It was not due to shyness at all as many women use to do. "There is unemployment, terrorism, illiteracy and political corruption in Pakistan, is it so?" "Yes." "And you want to change that situation?" "I am very afraid of the word, 'change'." I said, "I am not that much strong to control the conditions you have mentioned. Pakistan is a country of 130 million people in which hardly 15% use to read the paper and hardly 5% of the people would be true to their profession. We need money, time, energy and a long life just to move that society and, life in my country is cheaper than the cost of potatoes and onions." "Are you do not corrupt being a civil servant?" "No. I'm not." "Are you not given the opportunity, or you won't do that?" "Both things are wrong. In fact, my life is an exceptional since childhood. I want changes in my profession too.

That's why I am here." "Are you impressed of the beauty of nature beside the studies in Norway?" I looked into her blue eyes. "Tell me please." She pulled me with shirt. "Come closer to me." I was drunk but controlled. "There are many liberal women here who can come closer to you and sleep with you." She said and I became quit. Was there any complex in me to come closer to any Norwegian woman like many other foreigners? "Why did you come?" "I don't have come closer to you just because of your blue eyes and blond hair." "Then why?" "There is the reflection of my lost beloved in you." "I am a different person from that dead woman." "I am pulled by that different person. I want to cross the pains of that killed woman. I want to kill them." "Your action is very sweet to me." I looked in her eyes again. "Can you see in my eyes for half an hour?" I said and she looked at me. To see into blue eyes is like to see in the clean sky. "Then why did you marry again?" "Because I fell in love again." "What do you think about her?" "I need her. She is lovely. I can't live with any woman other than her for a long time in this whole world." We talked about many issues and when masters of the pub were about to close the door then we also left it. The cold breeze entered the nerves of our bodies while we left the heated pub. I saw her from her back and hugged her. I kissed her on the shoulders, cheeks and, I don't know where and how many times. "We are dishonest to your wife and Herald." "I don't think so." "If Herald sees us in this situation, he might kill both of us." "Doesn't he have other women friends?" "He is a honest man." She said," If somebody makes love in Pakistan on roads, what will they do to them?" "The girl will be ousted from the society and will be treated as an immoral human being. But the man will be comfortable with himself after a few days." When I left her pressed hand, I felt as if the silence had descended into my soul after a thunderstorm. We walked silently for a long while. At last Catherine saw a taxi and sat in it. "Sleep well." She said as she sat in the taxi.

Norway's Independence Day

The next day in Oslo, it was all colorful. The sun was shining. A channel on TV at that hotel talked about the whole city. The TV displayed a park of statues, which was known as "Vigilant Park". I desired to see it so eagerly and went there. While entering I saw the statue of a nude boy smiling like a rose. The statue was full of life. I kept looking at smile of the boy for a long time. Alas! Someone could make the picture of my feeling over this child. In this park, there are several beautiful and attractive statues on its right and left, which shows the human freedom, love, sorrow and other different human expressions. Sun of the May had given prominence to those statues even more. There were many tourists seen on that day in the park. A woman I saw was feeding the birds. There were many statues expressing human love and in Scandinavia, human love with body expressions was uniquely expressed. I saw a man and a woman kissing each other, hugging. Somewhere man loving intensely the woman's breast, looking greedily at woman's sexual organs. All that shown in the statues was in such a way that I started to believe that physical love was any how the most prominent expression among all the ways of expressing love. Many children were surrounded with a tree in one of the statues in the park. I appreciated the work of the artist. Later when I saw the way of making statues in Brussels (Belgium), I felt it was not so difficult to prepare them. They burned the mud and used different stones but to carve out the smile and, the meaningful eyes in a statue was really an art. It was marvelous as to how they presented the expressions in stony faces, sorrow, anguish, anger etc. and all that. The artist would have gone through many feelings while being at work and would have articulated and anticipated victorious smile when he had finished the work. I have seen a lot of galleries and museums of statues throughout Europe but there is no museum I could be inspired of more than the Vigilant Park in Oslo. After that I went to see the Viking ship museum. Viking is the name of that community on which the people of Norway and Iceland are proud of. They claim that the Vikings started shipping for the very first in history and they were the first who built the sea boats or ships prior to any other nation on earth.

There is a legend that the Norwegians claim, they were the only people who found America in the beginning. Their first made ships were on display in the museum. By seeing them one could feel the modern shipping measures that were known to them earlier. However, it can't be a fact that the measures used today were the same as Vikings used them, but many Norwegians don't admit that because they have a traditional attachment with the Vikings. Many pubs were crowded in the evening of Oslo that day. People were drinking beer with excitement. It was Saturday. Many couples were kissing each other being free from the hardship of the outgoing winter. There was a musical evening in center of the city. Many singers were singing either Norwegian or English songs. It was like an open-air theater just in the center from where many pubs and restaurants were linked and crowded. A group of children came to sing a song in very sweat rhythm. I intensely desired to have known the Norwegian language at the time. Alas! I wish I could understand the meaning of that song in those innocent voices. It is very rare that you find crowded people in Norway and those are the only sunny days when people come out of their houses as the snakes come from their caves. Birds use to sing and, the rays of sun on green grass seem to be twinkling waves. That Saturday in Oslo was one of those beautiful days. I came back to Trondheim and saw the last snowfall of the season in May. The people were surprised to witness snowing in May. I had to finish my project. There were a lot of parties because of the farewell days in Norway. Every day seemed to be the last day in that small but beautiful country. The most unforgettable day was May 17, which is Norway's Independence Day. It is celebrated with full zeal and excitement. The slogans and advertisements, which I saw on TV Pakistan's Independence Day, was in the similar way shown about Norway on 17th May. People were crazy to sing the national songs and jubilant in hoisting the country's flag atop their houses. How truly these people love their land and how religiously they remember their struggle of freedom in their happy moments and enjoy their economic stability. Can't this spirit of patriotism be equally distributed among all nations of the world? It was 17th and the center of Trondheim was flashing with a variety of dresses. Everybody was wearing his local dress. The sun was shining. People were seen very happy from different ways. I was roaming about with my wife in the city. We saw the Norwegian flag in almost everyone's hands and desired to have one. We ran to buy one, but they were all sold. My wife saw two flags in one small girl's hands and, she thought to ask for one from her. "You have two flags. Can you give me one?" she said to the small girl. The girl didn't reply but the grandmother accompanying her brought us one. "Where from are you?" The old lady asked. "Pakistan." "Why do you have so much interest in Norwegian flag?" "We have lived here for a year. We feel as if this country is our second home." We walked through center of the city having a small baby in its prompt. In a short time, the citizens started to celebrate their Independence Day. Today we came to know that how many Associations, Academies, Clubs and Groups are there in this city. Among them some were the Associations of Engineers, Architects, and other professionals and, some were of old people to take care of their old age. Some clubs belonged to commercial people as of those who sell carpets, garments etc. It was surprising to see a club of mustaches named; "Trondheim club of Mustaches." Every group displayed their own professional performance. We, three were running around the crowded groups in the city where we had a son, and I was trained in such a way that I came to know how really a nation should behave and how things change globally. We on that day saw freshness on every face. After some days when I saw professor Bratteland and his wife in their national dress, I felt how elevated one feels about himself if he works for his nation and be proud when he sees some results. When I saw the hoisted flag atop their house, I asked the professor, "Is it due to a sense of a tradition or just an entertainment, which prompted you to hoist this flag?" "There are many national days in this country. We don't care about other days but never forget to hoist the flag on 17th May." Said professor Bratteland. There weren't any important things in that party except that this was the last party during our course. Due to some reasons, there will be no course on this subject in the next year hence this year was very important for professor Bratteland who was running this course for last 15 years. He said many nice things in his last speech but there were a few words, which I would never forget; "Remember the developed countries can never develop your lands. It is only you who can develop your lands." I had to come back to Sindh with these inspiring words where an ethnic organization had paralyzed the civic life by conducting strikes four days a week. I met two other main personalities in that party; those were Elizabeth and, Tore. Elizabeth belonged to Uganda and Tore was a Norwegian, both were married in Norway and, were living in Trondheim. Elizabeth was dark black as Ugandans usually are and she had a feeling about her son who was born in Norway and was facing many troubles due to small degree of racism in this country as the locals in Norway didn't own her child. Being a mother, she was very sad on that issue. "Norwegians have seen 400 years of slavery. They face oppressive winters, which come along with snowy storms. It is very natural to be rude for them. You should comment on them only after looking at their background." I told Elizabeth in the party.

"You are actually touching the real nerve." Said tore. Elizabeth was a very frank and friendly woman. She was a student of psychology and was working on the project named; "The reactions of foreigners in Norway." With this reference she always admitted that the Norwegians are very straight, but they will take time to be mingled with foreigners. Every foreigner who was living in Moholt had the same complaint but in last days, there was a wise reply, when I asked my Chinese intelligent friend, Chin, "After having live for two years in Norway, what is your brief comment about this country?" "I like to live here." Said Chin, "I have lived in America and Australia, but you don't feel inferiority complex in this country." This way everyone has his own idea. Everyone comes with his own social background from his country and becomes foreigner somewhere in the world hence I always think that every foreigner has his own psychology. He develops a change in his thinking when he lives on any foreign land and presents the reaction which is mixed with his own country's background. The world would be running like this, no one can have life to his fullest satisfaction although he is always looking for. It is in the nature of a human being that he is always languishing for truth and equality, but he never finds them completely.

Last Days in Trondheim

In the last week of May, suddenly the snow vanished, and the sun came out. It was always the day; the night was not seen for many days. It was only the sunset time spanned over 23 hours between 110 and 10 in the late hours. Since Norway is very near to the Arctic Circle hence midnight sun appears there, in which the sun sets in for only a few moments and then appears again. This is clearer in the northern cities of Norway like Tromso. Due to this midnight sun, people in south consider north as the part of the world having six months day and six months night. Although that observation is not correct because this only happens at the poles. Since Trondheim is in the center of Norway hence midnight sun is not seen here. There is a bridge built in the cradle of Trondheim along with Nidelva River. I could see only one week of full bright sunshine and used to walk along with the walkways of that bridge for many kilometers in that week. People used to take sunbathe on the grass, which was grown along with the walkway. It was my first experience to see the people without clothes lying on the grass along with bridge built on a very beautiful river in Norway. Some people play badminton and, some others play with Pepsi caps. To see the nude woman lying on the grasses in Norway provoked my feelings about woman hence I used to watch them while walking. A nude woman walking or lying on the grass is like a mobile statue sculptured by Michael Anglo. When the summer comes, everything uses to grow, and it is green everywhere. Those paths where there was only snow or icy roads and, we were used to slip on them every day were now grassy. I felt, as if one day when I will open my eyes from a long sleep of darkness, Trondheim would become a bright city of beauty. I used to hear many languages of birds from the trees while walking towards the fjord. I don't know what type of attraction there was in the fjord so that whenever I walked towards it, a strange force would develop in my nerves. A small quantity of snow was seen far away on the mountains and the water of sea had changed its color. It was now blue like sky. The whole Norway is white in winter, but the people become crazy when they enjoy the summer of a very few days. They used to run every uncaring of their clothes and cold. In the last week in Norway when I had finished my project and my wife also had gone to London, I had nothing to do but to enjoy the summer and wait to see the motherland. Everyone seemed to be bright; people in Moholt had found their own fun and frolics. Some used to cook on the grass and some others used to play Volleyball or badminton up to 12 0' clock in the night (which was not a night in fact). Whenever I opened the window, I saw people playing or lying on the grass. Guri was the only our Norwegian friend in Moholt of whose whereabouts we used to know. It was light now up to 11 0' clock in the night in Moholt and just a little darkness appeared from 11 to 1 0' clock. One day Guri was coming back from cycling at 10 0' clock in the evening and I was also coming back from a long walk that we met at telephone booth in Moholt. She laughed at me; I don't know why? According to my wife Guri doesn't like Pakistani society. The reason is not known. I have observed that Muslims from Pakistan react rather adversely on Norwegian society as compared to other Muslim countries. Pakistani Muslims, living in Trondheim were in their behavior more fundamentalist than any other Pakistani I have seen throughout world. There was an artistic picture in my house. Many Pakistanis did not like it and, whenever they came in my house, they wanted it to be removed from the wall. A man and a woman are about to kiss each other in it. Guri used to talk on these issues very freely. She always praised Indian society more than any other Asian country.

"Hi!" she called from a long distance. "How are you?" I asked her. "Fine. How is your wife in London?" "I hope she is better than me." She was wearing a small nicker and a shirt. Her skin is like wheat. People here not having the white skin are also proud of their different color. "We will miss you in Pakistan. If you find any opportunity to come over there, please do come." I said. "I have heard that those who have the Indian visa, can't have the Pakistani visa or vice versa." "I don't know about it. It may be correct because both countries don't have good relations. Kashmir issue is the main point of conflict in between them." I said to her. She was walking along with me carrying the bicycle. I told her I shall be leaving Trondheim within a few days. It should be remembered that Guri was married but was separated by husband, 'Michael' of Ghana. About separation in Norway, there is a law that if any one of the couples wants divorce, the pair should be left to live separately for two years to finally decide for the divorce. They live separately for two years and share their children. If they don't decide anyway in those two years, then it will automatically be counted as divorce. Guri was not agreeing for divorce in this case. We came to know that Michael was single yet and, he didn't have any, girlfriend. "Have you forgotten about Michael now?" I asked a personal question from Guri after a long pause. She didn't reply. This nation was enjoying weather in summer and was not thinking about these problems. "Where is he nowadays?" I asked again. "We don't care about anybody in the summer because we enjoy life in this month after a long harsh winter of 11 months. However, Michael is in the city now. He takes Jacob every Friday and leaves him on Sunday." She told, "Now we are completing the time of separation and it is to be divorced. I have finished my course in Trondheim and am shifting to Oslo." "What will you do there?"

"That means you are leaving Trondheim with us." She was quiet. We walked to my room and said goodbye to each other. I had a permanent sad feeling for leaving Trondheim because it will never be possible to be so close to nature in Pakistan as in Trondheim and, I have been exercising that feeling in my soul so that on last day it should not give more pain. We went to see professor Bratteland's cabin in sea before two days of leaving the Trondheim and passed the whole day there. This cabin is built on an ideal place at two hours' drive. The clean blue water of the sea is seen through cabin in the cradle of fjord and a small island is seen as if child lying in the cradle. That island had enhanced the beauty of sea from the cabin. People are also seen on the island. There are two rooms in the cabin, one is bedroom and, the other is a living room. There is a veranda from where the sea appeared elevated, and a small microscope put on the floor of veranda from which we could enjoy the half-naked tourists on the island. I had taken the stock of beer for the whole day, but no one was accompanying me. I felt the students were now only waiting to return to their lands and, now they had nothing to enjoy in Norway. Mrs. Brit, Bratteland's wife, accompanied me. "Norway is your second home now." Brit said, "Whenever you will see the news about Norway on TV or you will see a Norwegian ship anchored at your port, you will miss it and, you will remember a good part of your life at that time." Both the husband and wife along with their son were working to fix the curtains in their cabin and they were doing a cement work in the veranda by themselves. Everybody had brought his lunch with him. My Sri Lankan fellows were very friendly and loving, they also helped the professor in the repair of his house. Here in Norway everybody does the repair work in his house by himself because the labor is very expensive. "He always keeps you busy." Said Brit again, "Why the developing countries don't remove corruption from their countries and take some measures?"

"The corruption can't be removed unless there is a population control." Said Thoufeeque. "And also, the politics of corruption is stopped." "Governments make such policies to derive people towards corruption." I said, "It is easy to blame the corruption of developing countries, but it is not easy to remove it if you are part of that society." Professor was listening that discussion quietly and didn't comment up to the last moment. I had seen a surprising gentleness in this man. I used to see the sea from cabin most of the time and, enjoyed it. The temperature was about 10c at that time. The cabin was open from all directions hence there was loud roar of wind. Up to the last day I had kept wearing the leather jacket which I had bought from Pakistan and now it had bored me. "It was 36c last year in this cabin." Professor told," and we were sweating." "You have now the experiences of both weathers, cold and hot. Which one do you think is easier to fight back?" Brit asked. "To face the hot weather is easier." A Sri Lankan fellow said. "Why?" Brit asked. "Because you can throw your clothes in heat and, it is difficult to face the storms of winter because then you have to stay most of the time in house." He said again. "Yes, but you can't throw away your skin in the heat?" said professor Bratteland and everyone laughed. The sun was shining when I was leaving Trondheim and, I was coming to airport in the taxi. I passed through Nidelva Bridge and stored a colorful memory in my soul. I was sure that I would never come again to this city where I had passed a brief part of my life. I thought I could never become a NORAD fellow when I passed through NTH. I saluted this excellent university which had trained me at such a level which I couldn't achieve during my 30 years life. This university updated me in my subject as well as it created a global mindset in me. I met with many people from different cultures and attended a lot of seminars over human rights. I was coming back to my country. Pinkish smile was prominent on their faces, and I remembered that day when I entered for the first time in this city. The nature had absorbed me to itself, and I was taking thousands of memories with me while leaving this country. There were many characters, which were still incomplete. I thought every character is incomplete in this world and, he leaves this country in me like the fresh air, snow peaked mountains, lakes, rivers and fjords, the chirping of birds in trees, the fighting for life with the oppressive weather and struggle! One can ask everything from nature but time!

Author's published books:

1 Hik Kaenra Jo mout (Death of a Coward) Short Stories and a novelette in Sindhi

2- Bay Darje jee zindagi (Life of a second-class citizen) newspaper articles in Sindhi

3- Aurat Bina Siyaro (winter without woman) Travelogue of Norway in Sindhi

4- Historical Interviews – Interviews of Pakistani authors in English

Author's coming books:

1. Travels to Rome and Roman Empire

2. Autobiography

Printed in Great Britain
by Amazon

25110161R00059